the JOURNEY BACK to

Eden

Also by Glen G. Scorgie

A Call for Continuity
The Challenge of Bible Translation (coeditor)

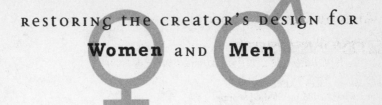

RESTORING THE CREATOR'S DESIGN FOR
Women AND **Men**

the JOURNEY BACK to

Eden

GLEN G. SCORGIE

ZONDERVAN™

GRAND RAPIDS, MICHIGAN 49530 USA

ZONDERVAN™

The Journey Back to Eden
Copyright © 2005 by Glen G. Scorgie

Requests for information should be addressed to:
Zondervan, *Grand Rapids, Michigan 49530*

Library of Congress Cataloging-in-Publication Data

Scorgie, Glen G.
  The journey back to Eden : restoring the Creator's design for women and men /
Glen G. Scorgie.—1st ed.
     p. cm.
  Includes bibliographical references.
  ISBN-10: 0-310-25990-8
  ISBN-13: 978-0-310-25990-9
  1. Sex role—Religious aspects—Christianity.   2. Women—Religious aspects—
Christianity.   3. Men (Christian theology).   I. Title.
  BT708.S36 2005
  270'.082—dc22
                                                                    2005015667

Interior design by Tracey Walker

Printed in the United States of America

05 06 07 08 09 10 11 12 /❖ DCI/ 10 9 8 7 6 5 4 3 2 1

to claire, catherine, and sarah —
each dedicated at birth
to the only one greater than herself

Contents

List of Diagrams

Acknowledgments

Writing is rarely undertaken alone, or completed alone. My biggest debt is to my wife and daughters, who permitted this manuscript to be table talk, endured rhetorical deliveries of many parts of it, and encouraged me along in the creative process. Unfortunately, daughter Claire's proposed title, *Jesus Was from Venus Too*, never survived the editorial cut.

I am grateful for both the affirmations and criticisms (precious are the wounds of a friend) of Mark Strauss, Thorsten Moritz, Jim Smith, Tom Correll, Dan Watson, LeRon Shults, Craig Keener, Linda Belleville, Bill Webb, Stan Gundry, and my discerning editors Paul Engle and Greg Clouse. Judi Bailey, Mary-Lou Bradbury, and Francoise Anderson at Bethel Seminary San Diego provided indispensable support. Some people have influenced me through their writings more than the endnotes attest. These include Ron Youngblood, R. T. France, Kevin Giles, Stan Grenz, Rebecca Merrill Groothuis, Richard Longenecker, Barbara MacHaffie, Dennis Preato, Rosemary Radford Ruether, and Bill Webb.

A special group, mainly Bethel Seminary students, carefully read earlier versions of the manuscript, and then came together to discuss it one evening in our home. The group included Robert Bradshaw, Alice and Tom Trotter, David and Angela McKinney, Brian Tallman, Cathy Metts, Jeff and Anna Lawton, Donald Liu, J. B. Preato, Kathryn and Etienne de Bruin, Cliff and Sue Olson, Karen Maczka, Lisa Reynolds, and Christie Nielsen. There was poetic justice in how they sent back the professor's work all marked up in red ink!

Some of this material has been presented at Schloss Mittersill, an evangelical study center near Salzburg, Austria; to our local chapter of Christians for Biblical Equality; and in a series of lectures, copresented with Mark Strauss, at College Avenue Baptist Church in San Diego. I learned a great deal from participants on all these occasions.

Finally, I am grateful to Bethel Seminary and its provost, Leland Eliason, for a sabbatical reprieve from teaching duties. Without it, this project would probably still be languishing. Not everyone I have acknowledged agrees with everything in this book. Responsibility for the views expressed herein is mine alone. But the book is definitely better for everyone's contributions. Whenever we are able to *really* hear one another, we all move a bit closer to the light.

Introduction

HOW I came to write this book

In the nineteenth century the Slessor clan on my mother's side emigrated from Scotland to Canada, where they established themselves in rural Ontario as farmers, butchers, and eventually as General Motors car dealers. Without wishing to offend my extended family, I think it's safe to say that we have been a rather ordinary lot. Our most famous relative would definitely be my great-great-great aunt who, like other relatives, left Scotland, but in her case departed for Africa rather than Canada—as a pioneer United Presbyterian missionary to Calabar, the Biafran region of present-day Nigeria.

Mary Slessor (1848–1915) established herself first as a malaria survivor, and thereafter as an intrepid evangelist and champion of abandoned and orphaned children. Cut from the same cloth as so many other bold, entrepreneurial Victorian missionaries, she tended to take matters into her own hands, and over a long career often refused to acquiesce to the directives of mission-board bureaucrats back home. Since then she has figured large among the heroes of the evangelical missionary movement, alongside the likes of David Livingstone and Hudson Taylor.[1]

About twenty years ago we went to Dundee, Scotland, and visited a museum that contained a display in honor of Mary, our one famous Slessor relative. It portrayed her as a simple, young workingwoman from one of the city's Victorian jute mills (suppliers of sail cloth for the Royal Navy) who, through unusual willpower and strength of character, made something of herself on the international stage. Under a glass cover there in the museum lay her worn King James Bible, open to 1 Timothy 2. Beside the apostle Paul's famous words, "but I suffer not a woman to teach, nor to usurp authority over the man, but to be in silence," Mary had written in dull pencil her vigorous personal reaction. Evidently she had been offended, and wrote: "No, no,

Paul laddie. This will na' do!" I remember being amused at the time, but just a bit unsettled too. And the nagging feeling stuck with me for years. How could *the* Mary Slessor—*our* Mary Slessor—the missionary hero, have been so dismissive of, even patronizing toward, apostolic authority? I had to ask myself whether she really believed in the infallibility of Scripture.

The Women in My Life

Today I am blessed to be surrounded by a number of outstanding women. One is Kate, my life partner for the past quarter century, who is a professor at Azusa Pacific University here in southern California. The others are Claire, Catherine, and Sarah, our three young-adult daughters. Part of what makes me tick as a human being is a fierce love for these women. Like other parents in our age cohort, Kate and I have been trying to raise our daughters in a North American culture that is socially and spiritually toxic, especially for young women.[2] Messages come from every conceivable angle these days to convince them that they are ultimately objects, not persons, and that their worth (and best chances for love) lie in external considerations like appearance, clothes, and sexual availability.

We've looked to the evangelical church, our spiritual home, for help in this ongoing spiritual battle of values and identity formation, and are grateful for the help we have received. But as I've journeyed with the women in my life (and listened to the similar poignant stories of many gifted women in my seminary classes), I've come to recognize that the evangelical church far too often sends out negative, even devastating, messages to women today.

It's a known fact that the self-esteem of women is not high in our ecclesiastical circles, and there are reasons for this. Evangelical women are not yet being given an equal voice, they are not yet being invited in sufficient numbers into the key decision-making circles, and they are not yet being assigned the more visible ministry roles of teaching and leadership. Yet the plea of most women today is not merely, or even primarily, for an equal share of power. It is for something much deeper. It is for personal dignity and freedom, for respect and reciprocal affirmation as they, like men, seek to realize all the potential that God has already implanted, in nascent form, in their souls.

In a host of ways, including subtleties of social interaction about which good Christian men are often quite oblivious, evangelical women feel demeaned and diminished. When younger women (as well as older ones) can no longer resist the cumulative weight of such external messages, and when there are too few women in respected leadership roles to inspire their hope and sustain their resilience through example, they can capitulate. They can internalize the themes of patriarchy, and accept the lie that they belong to the weaker, more trivial and flawed version of humanity.

These socialization processes within the evangelical church have been going on (and been perpetuated, incidentally, by good people who love the Lord) for generations now, and they permanently condition and shape women. For it is simply impossible to restrict the functions of women in Christian community, with alleged divine sanction, without sending a signal that such restrictions make sense because women are less worthy in their essential nature. The earlier patriarchs of the Christian tradition, who consistently put down women, deserve credit for at least this: they grasped the logic that gender hierarchy as a social system cannot be sustained, or ultimately make sense, unless women really are inferior in nature and constitutionally unsuited to teach or lead men.

Seeing through New Eyes

It is one thing to study gender issues in a comfortably detached way. It is quite another thing to experience them through the pain and crises of faith of those closest to you. Some of my critics will immediately insist that I have just admitted to a biased perspective to this topic. They will suggest that this book can be dismissed as the product of someone whose thinking has been distorted by personal experience. They will argue that as Christians we must build our theology and ethics on the objective Word of God, not notoriously deceptive human subjectivity.

Let me acknowledge that I did not always think as I do now. I once held a traditional view on gender issues. But the pain of those I love, and persistent slights toward them, forced me to go back and reread Scripture with an open mind and heart. As I did, I became aware of things that I had not seen, or perhaps could not have seen, before. I began to view the biblical landscape through different eyes. It was a gradually dawning conversion of sorts. Of all people, evangelicals should give anyone with a testimony to having changed their mind at least the benefit of the doubt. Conversions, we know, can be good things!

Experience has always had something important to contribute to evangelical theological method. Wisdom is acquired in the crucible of life experience, and such wisdom is essential to correctly interpreting the Word of God. All the facts in the world are wasted if we do not have eyes to see and ears to hear. Experience is not always a liability. It can be a *wake-up call*, as the apostle Paul after his trip to Damascus would surely attest. Personal bias must never be allowed to distort the meaning of Scripture, nor be given a weight greater than that of Scripture itself. But vivid personal experience often helps to bring clarity to our understanding. It helps lift the veil of misunderstanding that accompanies the complacent acceptance of biased assumptions. All truth is God's truth, so every genuinely insightful experience we have will contribute positively to our understanding of what God is trying to say to us through Scripture.

From time to time we hear of a professional athlete—a fast-living multimillionaire who seems to have it all. But then one of his little children is diagnosed with leukemia. Suddenly everything changes for him. He has a new perspective. His priorities are different. He claims to have discovered what life is really all about. We do not dismiss such people as *biased* by their experience. Instead, we acknowledge that they have acquired deeper wisdom and insight.

My "conversion" on the gender issue has been the catalyst for a larger perceptual transformation. It has helped me finally *hear* the stories of so many women wounded by the very church they love and serve with sincerity. And I have begun to recognize patterns in the life stories shared by Christian women, whether young adults around our

kitchen table, able academics from Asia, outstanding retired missionaries, "directors" of children's and women's ministries, or gifted sem-
inarians with slim prospects for challenging ministry placement. A
hypothesis is vindicated by its explanatory power—by the degree to
which it makes sense of the facts. In my case, the authentic experience
of a few close to me has become a window into the much larger reality of the many.

I want the world to know that the gospel of Jesus Christ is good
news, and that it is *really* good news for women. And I want women
to be able to pick up just from the way Christians "do life," inside and
outside the church, that God is, well, *good for us*. There ought to be
no temptation for women to turn their backs on Christianity in order
to become all that they were meant to be. Women, those who consti-
tute fully half the population of this planet, with all its pain and
poverty and deceptive ideologies, need to know that the Spirit of Jesus
Christ is the most liberating, empowering, and fulfilling dynamic in
all of history. And I wish for them to see this truth embodied in the
everyday life of the community of faith, the church, which is meant to
be a prototype of the kingdom.

If Mary Slessor were to meet the apostle Paul, I can imagine that
they would hit it off rather well. They would soon be exchanging
notes on mission strategies, regaling each other with amazing stories
of risk and deliverance, and reveling in the power of the gospel. As
they warmed to each other, and their mutual respect deepened, Paul
might very well begin to refer to Mary as a real coworker, apostle, or
deacon—like he had other pioneer women leaders of his own day. He
definitely would *not* offer her a job as his secretary. And I can't help
but think that he would explain the true meaning and *authorial intent*
of his remarks in 1 Timothy 2 to Mary's satisfaction. What I don't
know is how he would take the news of the spin the church has put
on his comments for the past two millennia. His response to that
would be very interesting indeed.

CHAPTER 1

Tracing the Trajectory of the Spirit

a DISCERNING approach to SCRIPTURE

The ball is snapped. The quarterback backpedals into the pocket forming around him. There he sets up and waits, amid Richter scale–level collisions all around. Powerful opponents violently encroach. At the last possible second, he steps forward and forcefully launches a long bomb. The football soars into the sky on a magnificent arching trajectory, moving fast and spinning smoothly.

Downfield, the pass receiver has been zoned in on the ball from the moment it cleared the scrimmage line. Running hard, he instinctively calibrates its velocity, the angle of its rise, and even its spin. His "read" on the ball is everything. It determines whether he will catch up to it or watch it fall incomplete. With a quick head-fake he shakes the defender, adjusts his route, and strains for a spot in the far corner of the field. The ball is still nowhere near there, but from a quick shoulder glance he's confident that's where it's coming down. Seconds later he leaps high, draws the football to his chest, and tumbles gloriously into the end zone. Touchdown!

A large part of the art of pass receiving is being able to recognize where the ball is going *before* it gets there. A great receiver can predict a football's trajectory from near the point of release. This book is also about tracing a trajectory—another kind, the trajectory of the Holy Spirit. And it is not about football either, but something quite different and much more important: how men and women ought to stand in relationship to one another. Nevertheless the same principle applies.

We need to "read" the Spirit's trajectory, and recognize where God's Spirit is headed on the subject of gender relations.

All things considered, Christianity has been good for women. It has not been the mighty agent of gender oppression that it is sometimes made out to be. Still, contemporary Christians can hardly feel smug about the track record of our religious tradition. We live with the uncomfortable awareness that our faith has not been as affirming as it should have been, or as empowering for women as it certainly needs to be from now on.

This book is a call for a paradigm shift in the way many Christians still view men and women. In particular it is addressed to the emerging generation of Christians who wish the church could do more for women, but who until now have reluctantly assumed that loyalty to Scripture compels them to perpetuate a hierarchical view of gender relations. It invites such readers to see the biblical landscape through new eyes. To assist in such reappraisal, it traces the trajectory of the Spirit across the pages of Scripture and the annals of history. It explores the directional impulse of the Spirit, who is slowly but surely bringing us back to the personal wholeness and harmonious relationships that have largely eluded us as men and women since the fall.

A Vision of Equality, Freedom, and Mutuality

The thesis of this book is that the Holy Spirit is nudging the people of God today toward a fuller embrace of the gospel vision of gender equality, freedom, and mutuality. What do these three cornerstones of the gospel vision involve? Concerning the first, the church is slowly grasping the truth that women and men, though obviously not identical, are *equal* in every sense. There must no longer be an asterisk placed beside this affirmation of gender equality, no qualification whatsoever of this foundational truth. Neither men nor women are more or less inclined to sinfulness; we are perfectly equal in our sinning. Likewise, neither women nor men are more like God; we are peers in our God-likeness, dignity, and potential.

Freedom, the second ideal, means that every woman and man should be able to pursue their calling before God, with careful discernment of

DIAGRAM 1.1. The Trajectory of the Spirit through Time

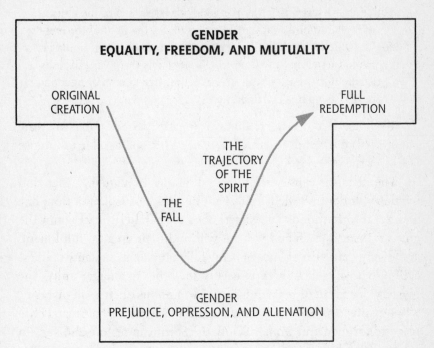

gifts and ability, of course, but without any restrictions on what their gender allows them to do. Exactly where such freedom might take men and women cannot be perfectly anticipated in advance; the adventurous experiment still has not reached its conclusion. The point is to wait and see what will happen in an atmosphere of complete Spirit-superintended freedom. It is possible that gender tendencies may emerge (perhaps even ones not totally dissimilar to the status quo). But when freedom is honored, such tendencies will be regarded as observed trends rather than imposed templates, and it will never be considered unnatural or abnormal for a woman or man to deviate from such statistical patterns. Anything less is gender profiling.

The church should be in the vanguard of this Spirit movement, not reluctantly bringing up the cultural rear. Recently Hans Küng insightfully observed:

Everything that indisputably manifests itself as un-freedom in the church is not a revelation of the good, clear essence of the church but a revelation of its dark, evil perversion. In the light of the message on which it bases itself, the church in its inner being should be a sphere of freedom. A church which proclaims the gospel of Jesus Christ shouldn't bring people servitude but freedom: "For freedom Christ has set us free" (Gal. 5:1).[1]

We must dare to believe that the Spirit is perfectly able to create communal order and peace without need for one gender to impose rule over the other.

The ideal for gender relations culminates in *mutuality*. Men and women will not find their fulfillment in estranged isolation from one another. Brotherhoods and sisterhoods on parallel tracks is not the answer. Instead, men and women will find their greatest fulfillment, and their greatest experience of being fully human, in a quality of interaction that welcomes and appreciates the other in a larger unity. The mystery of a mutually enriching and harmonious oneness in diversity, without any "bosses" or top-down control, is what God ultimately has in mind for men and women. Only the Spirit can restore and sustain such a desirable vision; thankfully, nothing more than the Spirit is required for it to become a reality.

The gospel is certainly about *more* than the healing of gender relations, but it is not about *less*. It is the good news of Christ's *comprehensive* solution to *all* the guilt, power, and horrific consequences of human sinfulness—including the prospect of eternal death. But such a wonderful gospel *includes* the promise of complete healing of the pain of dysfunctional gender relations. And it is to this particular aspect of the good news that we intend to direct our attention in this book.

An Estranged Daughter

Christianity has been a transforming influence on every society in which it has taken deep root. Through the positive influences of the Christian faith, the history of Western civilization has been a story of the gradual overthrow of oppressive political structures, the creation of more democratic alternatives, and the emergence of greater freedoms for all. The distinctive theology of the Protestant Reformation, particularly its liberating and exultant celebration of the priesthood of *all* believers, was a major stimulant to these impulses in Europe and beyond. Most Christians see God's providence in these liberating developments. They regard freedom as a central theme of the gospel, because Christ came to set captives free (Luke 4:18), and whom the Son sets free will be free indeed (John 8:36).

Yet progress has been slow. As late as 1775, there was still no truly democratic government in the United States. In Britain the right to a university education was restricted to Anglicans until near the end of the nineteenth century. The practice of human slavery was tolerated in the United States until the 1860s. The many residual inequities after Emancipation in America required a civil rights movement in the 1960s, and that struggle continues today.

Alongside these developments have risen female expectations for a voice, greater personal dignity, equal opportunity, and individual autonomy. Certain gains for American women stand out as landmarks, such as the legal right to own property, to attend university, and, with women's suffrage in 1920, to vote. Yet vestiges of gender inequality still survive in our culture. The aim of contemporary feminism is to liberate women from these remaining forms of oppression and to promote their full equality and liberated participation in society. At the heart of this movement is a desire to affirm the full legitimacy of women (not least, to women themselves), and to demonstrate that their abilities and competencies are equal, not inferior, to those of men.

This advance toward greater female equality and freedom is having an unsettling effect on the status quo. Traditional roles are becoming more flexible, while accepted patterns of family decision-making are coming under review. The phenomenon of "uneasy manhood" has emerged as males look for role clarification in the face of the demise of the old, familiar models.[2] Some Christians, looking back with nostalgia to more stable days gone by, blame most of the social challenges and ills of our society on the "wholly inappropriate" aspirations of women today. They view the feminist movement as a sinister way of tempting Christians to parrot the destructive values of secular society.

The reality, however, is that the roots of contemporary feminism are found in Christianity itself. It is no accident that feminism emerged from a cultural environment profoundly influenced by Christ, for only from such a heritage could it have acquired its vision of female empowerment and gender equality. The roots of organized feminism long predate the turbulent 1960s. They trace back to the nineteenth century, when evangelical women successfully fought slavery, demanded the right to vote, changed unjust laws, organized armies of philanthropic volunteers, and pioneered in missionary endeavors all over the world. Christian feminism predates secular feminism. We should not view the latter as an alien movement, but as Christianity's own wounded and estranged daughter.

The secular feminist movement is definitely flawed. Nevertheless, it is a cry of the human spirit against attitudes and behaviors that are an affront to women as divine image-bearers. There is something of God—the God who hears the cry of the oppressed—in the contemporary longing of women for a better way. The situation we face today is both a crisis and an opportunity for the body of Christ. The quest for female equality and freedom should be supported by the church, even as parts of it are being purified. When all is said and done, Christianity originally birthed the feminist impulse, and it is not characteristic of good Christians to renounce their offspring, even if some of them have become prodigal.

Evangelical Polarization on Gender

The gender egalitarian impulse today is compelling Christians to go back and examine our assumptions about God's will for the sexes, and our views of how men and women ought to relate to one another. Evangelical opinion has coalesced into two broad and competing responses. While these two perspectives are identified by various labels, the most common self-designations are *complementarian* and *egalitarian*. Each side has more polemic labels for the other, but generally the complementarian and egalitarian designations prevail. Both sides acknowledge the unqualified authority of Scripture. Both claim to affirm the equality in nature and essence of men and women, and both seek God's best for women and men alike.[3]

The pivotal difference of opinion between the two is whether or not the Bible teaches a *normative pattern* for gender relations—an order or *gender template* that inevitably shakes down into certain restrictions on the roles and functions that women should perform. Complementarians hold that the male has a unique and God-given leadership role to perform; for them, the essence of maleness is to lead benevolently, and the essence of femaleness is to affirm, nurture, and receive male strength and leadership.[4] By contrast, egalitarians deny the desirability of, or need for, differentials of power and freedom in gender relations. Instead, they believe, God's design is ultimately to overcome all the oppressive, estranging consequences of sin in male-female relationships. Among other things, this will require the dismantling of hierarchy, so that men and women can be reconciled in a grace-filled mutuality.

This vision celebrates gender difference. However, it maintains that gender relations should be free from preconditions and limitations that might restrict an individual's right to determine how he or she will live and serve in a given relationship or organization. Each uniquely gifted man and woman should be at liberty to find their best way of relating to others and of living in the world. Neither generalizations about gender, nor gender profiling, have any place in such a vision. Prejudgments about what constitutes an acceptable or unacceptable gender role inevitably generate iron templates that restrict individual freedom and crush the human spirit. On the other hand, when men and women are allowed to relate to one another in acknowledged equality, complete freedom, and genuine love, we will be able to stand back and witness the mystery of humanity as male and female unfolds before our eyes. This is the egalitarian vision in a nutshell, and also the viewpoint of this book.

Traditionally, Christians have assumed that the Bible affirms gender hierarchy, and there is general acknowledgment on both sides that patriarchal thinking does color parts of the biblical text. However, many Christians today are increasingly troubled by the traditional hierarchical interpretation. They see the damage it is doing to the credibility of the gospel, and the pain and low self-esteem it seems to be inducing in so many Christian women. Still, they are convinced that their allegiance to the Scripture obliges them to retain a hierarchical paradigm for gender relations. They see no alternative short of abandoning the authority of the Bible. If it were up to them, they say, they would be egalitarians, but their hands are tied; Scripture gives them no choice. In more conservative Christian circles it is widely assumed that one has to choose between egalitarian ideals and biblical faithfulness.

This book contests such an assumption. Evangelical egalitarians subscribe to the authority of the Bible every bit as much as complementarians. The real difference between us and our complementarian brothers and sisters is not our respective doctrines of Scripture, which are essentially the same. It is about our respective approaches to the content of the Bible we both regard as authoritative. The real issue between the two camps is not the doctrine of biblical infallibility but how best to practice biblical *interpretation*.

Three Essential Tasks of Bible Interpretation

If the egalitarian view is ever to gain ground in the evangelical community, its compatibility with a high view of Scripture must be demonstrated. This is as it should be, for fidelity to the Bible is at the very heart of historic evangelical identity. Truly evangelical egalitarians will never want to challenge the truthfulness of Scripture. They are as committed to biblical authority as any of their opponents. But they do challenge some aspects of traditional *interpretation*, and they commend their alternative viewpoint by pursuing three important tasks—which I call the *clarifying* task, the *restrictive* task, and the *discerning* task.

The first of these tasks is to *clarify* the correct meaning of biblical statements on gender. This approach assumes that Scripture does contain concepts and principles relevant to gender, and that these ought to be applied faithfully by the people of God today. For example, it bears pointing out that the Hebrew term for Eve (in Genesis 2) as a help to Adam meant that she was a helpful *equal partner* rather than an underling to fix his meals and bring him his slippers. By means of this clarifying approach we seek to ensure that everyone understands exactly what the Bible is really saying. In some instances this work will involve highlighting biblical texts and truths that Christians have tended to overlook. In many cases this work will show that the Bible is not as patriarchal as traditional readers have made it out to be.

The second task is to demonstrate that some biblical texts that have traditionally been regarded as normative for all time were in fact applicable only to the unique cultural situations they addressed. This line of interpretation puts a fence around qualifying biblical passages so that their application is *restricted* to local contexts in historically distant times—including, for example, calls for female head-coverings, the practice of foot washing, and greeting other believers with a "holy kiss" (Rom. 16:16). If the first hermeneutical task is one of clarifying gender norms, the second task is restricting or setting aside biblical material that is not, nor was ever meant to be, applicable to our circumstances today.

Egalitarians pursuing these first two tasks have actually developed a number of compelling arguments in favor of gender equality. They have convincingly demonstrated that some traditional interpretations are in error. But evidence of hierarchical thinking and attitudes is too deeply embedded within Scripture itself to be completely cleared up by these means alone. Even the apostolic writers encouraged acquiescence to the hierarchical structures of their day (including patriarchy) for the sake of the gospel's reputation. To some extent we can accept that, but what is lacking is evidence that the inspired writers were completely aware of, and sensitive to, the unfair burden this accommodating approach placed on the shoulders of slaves, women, and other less empowered members of the community. Clearly the apostles were concerned that in Christian relationships the harshness of patriarchy be mellowed and that relations become more benevolent. It is less clear that in gender matters the "finalized ethic" toward which the gospel ultimately points was always a top priority for them, or, in some cases perhaps, even fully grasped.

For these reasons we commend a third task involved in correctly handling the Word of God, and intend to employ it in what follows here.[5] This approach has been described as a developmental, progressive, or redemptive movement hermeneutic (a hermeneutic is simply an approach to interpreting the Bible). It is the effort to discern the overall direction the church is being led as the Spirit unfolds God's will in a progressive way. Scripture's teaching on gender relations can be envisioned in two ways: *static* or *teleological*. The static option is inert—not moving. By contrast, the teleological is going somewhere— it is purpose-driven. The static vision locks the Christian community into the gender norms prevailing at the time the New Testament was written. The latter discerns a path from tragedy to redemption, a process to which we are called to contribute. It attempts to discern the movement of the Spirit as God continues to lead the church forward along a vector established by the central impulses of the gospel.

This generates the *discerning* task of proper hermeneutics. It focuses on a goal, a not-yet-realized endpoint toward which the Bible is moving. It considers the concept of progressive revelation to be the best way to account for biblical directives, not to mention certain biblical silences, which would otherwise be problematic. Progressive revelation simply means that God gradually unfolds his will and ways more clearly over time—the light gets brighter as one moves forward. It is the basis for why some Christians now occasionally eat pork, although the Old Testament prohibits it. It explains why Bible-believing Christians today abstain from stoning their rebellious teenagers, even though the Old Testament law at one point recommends that they should. In the end, pursuing this discerning task of interpretation will enable us to see that gender egalitarianism is not a concession to be cleverly wrestled from Scripture. Rather, it is the vision toward which its inspired contents actually point.

The Trajectory of the Spirit

Here then, in summary form, is the vision that energizes the redemptive movement approach to interpreting the Bible—a vision that will be fleshed out in the rest of the book. It begins with the wonder and mystery of the God who existed before time as a Trinitarian fellowship of divine love. It sees the Holy Trinity revealed as a unity of three persons of equal God-ness, joined in a way that makes hierarchical structure and control among the persons unnecessary and inappropriate. It is this triune God whom we humans are to "image" in all our interactions, and preeminently in our relationships as male and female.

God's original design for full equality and mutuality in gender relations—a design revealed in the first few chapters of Genesis—was perverted by the fall. Sin introduced toxic gender dynamics of oppression and alienation, which have become entrenched in all human societies. God's original intentions for gender deteriorated, and the ensuing negative patterns have become universally reinforced by patriarchal ideologies.

Ever since, however, the Spirit of God has been at work to redeem this dysfunctional situation, to liberate humanity from every remainder of prejudice and oppression, and to restore the original design of gender equality, freedom, and mutuality. This redemptive work began modestly and is proceeding slowly. The relatively primitive times in which the Old Testament was written have been appropriately designated an age of patriarchy. Women had very limited spheres of influence and few rights or opportunities. Male privilege was rampant and unquestioned during those centuries, and the pages of the Old Testament reflect that reality.

As the inspired pages of Scripture indicate, God's revelations to the ancient people of Israel provisionally accommodated prevailing assumptions about gender. Some Mosaic legislation and prophetic messages softened the harsher injustices of prevailing patriarchal practices, but for the most part the system was allowed to persist. The seeds of the kingdom took root in patriarchal soil without initially disrupting that soil very much. Plotting the trajectory of the Spirit through the Old Testament must begin with seeing that the way things were is not the way God intends them to be.

The high-water mark of biblical revelation, and the zenith of God's plan of redemption, was the incarnation of Jesus Christ. The Gospels portray him as teaching God's truths with unprecedented clarity, revealing the heart of God, and modeling the new humanity for everyone to see. It was not only what Jesus said but how he related to women that was revolutionary. His ministry was characterized by a bold new egalitarian attitude.

The remainder of the New Testament builds on the work Jesus began and the truth he proclaimed. Many of the practices of the early church were faithful extensions of Christ's own attitudes toward women. Nonetheless, New Testament church practice did not always reflect as strongly and consistently as Jesus did the trajectory of the Spirit on gender issues. The proclamation of the gospel was once again accommodated to the realities of the contemporary context—in this instance, those of Palestinian Judaism and the larger Roman Empire.

Like the books of the Old Testament, the writings that became the New Testament are "God-breathed" (2 Tim. 3:16) and are therefore trustworthy and authoritative for Christians. At the same time we must recognize that New Testament writers, especially the apostle Paul, occasionally counseled compliance with reigning views of gender in order to maximize social acceptance of the gospel message itself. So it is that one of our greatest challenges is to discern the trajectory of the Spirit through the pages of the New Testament.

The more accurately we discern the Spirit's direction back then, the more reliably we can extrapolate the Spirit's will concerning gender issues in our day. As realists we expect that gender alienation and inequality will persist in our fallen world; it will be difficult to root out. At the same time we believe that the church is called to be a prototype of the coming kingdom of God; it is intended to be out front in the movement back to Eden. How we relate to one another as male and female is destined to reflect (or image) again the triune God's own inner life of loving mutuality. Ultimately, then, the Spirit's trajectory is pointing us back to a renewed likeness to God.

Seeing How the Bible Moves Forward

Dr. Laura Schlessinger has been a popular radio personality for years now. She dispenses curt, no-nonsense advice to those who dare to call her nationally syndicated show. Dr. Laura happens to be Jewish, and strongly believes that her Hebrew Bible (the Christian Old Testament) is a rich repository of divine wisdom for successful living. I have in my possession a fictitious letter to Dr. Laura, by someone pretending to seek contemporary advice on how to practice certain Old Testament laws. The person inquires: "When I burn a bull on the altar as a sacrifice, I know it creates a pleasing odor for the Lord (Lev. 1:9). The problem is my neighbors. They claim the odor is not pleasing to them. How should I deal with this?"

Tongue in cheek, the anonymous letter goes on, "I would like to sell my daughter into slavery, as it suggests in Exodus 21:7. In this day and age, what do you think would be a fair price for her?" Just one more—"I have a neighbor who insists on working on the Sabbath. Exodus 35:2 clearly states he should be put to death. Am I morally obligated to kill him myself?" In its humorous way the letter makes an important point about how we should handle the Bible.

DIAGRAM 1.2. The Relationship of the Old and New Testaments to the Trajectory of the Spirit

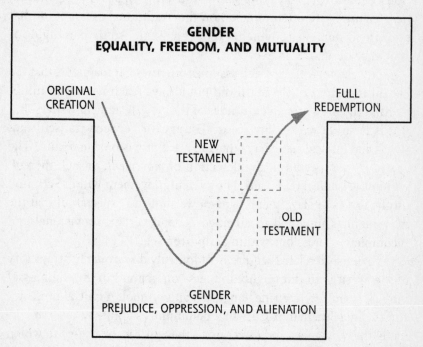

**GENDER
EQUALITY, FREEDOM, AND MUTUALITY**

ORIGINAL CREATION

FULL REDEMPTION

NEW TESTAMENT

OLD TESTAMENT

GENDER
PREJUDICE, OPPRESSION, AND ALIENATION

Evangelicals in the past have welcomed the principle of progressive revelation to deal with awkward portions of the Old Testament text. We believe God no longer wants us to annihilate unbelievers—man, woman, and child—or stone to death our own rebellious teenagers, even though this was once the "biblical" way of doing things. The approach to Bible interpretation which we are recommending extends the progressive principle into the New Testament text itself. According to this paradigm, it is not appropriate to view every New Testament statement as an ultimate and finalized expression of the driving force of the Spirit's prompting within it. The traditional view assumes that Scripture contains a permanently binding template for gender relations, a template built by collating all the scriptural statements relevant to the topic. This widely held view assumes that the apostolic writings of the New Testament consistently express the height of insight into God's plan for gender relations. Even the clarifying and restricting tasks of egalitarian hermeneutics are often pursued on this traditional assumption that all New Testament statements reflect a single, static paradigm for gender relations.

The teleological approach assumes otherwise. It maintains that the ethical trajectory of the Spirit did not always reach its perfect fulfillment in the priorities and attitudes of the New Testament writers. But if this is so, how then are we to distinguish between transcultural truths and biblical statements that are more provisional in nature? The answer lies above all in the detection of *movement*, or lack thereof, within the biblical text itself. The evident movement within Scripture on the topics of slavery and women warrant the expectation that the movement is intended to advance beyond certain provisional and incomplete expressions within Scripture itself.

Obviously a related requirement for truly discerning the trajectory of the Spirit is to thoroughly immerse one's mind in the richness of biblical narrative, doctrine, language, and symbol. A crucial prerequisite to any Christian or Christian community's ability to discern correctly the movement and direction of the Spirit is the degree to which they sense the flow, and are able to enter into the thought-world, of the Bible. In this way, and only this way, will we be able to recognize which interpretations are consistent with the whole of Christian truth.

The best preparation for discerning the direction of the Spirit is to have one's heart and mind continually "baptized" in the Word of God and its grand story of redemption.[6]

Some readers may react to this proposal with reservations that go something like this: "I am concerned that such an approach will allow devious people to invent what they want the Bible to mean. It will allow them to make unrestricted and purely subjective judgments about what is right and wrong. It will quickly undermine the authority of Scripture altogether."

N. T. Wright, a leading biblical scholar from England, offers a helpful response to such concerns. He compares the people of God today to a drama troupe that has discovered a long-lost Shakespearean play. There's a slight problem though. Part of the final act, a section near the end, is missing. If the troupe hopes to perform this masterpiece with integrity, it will have to imaginatively infer, from many clues in the text and from what they know of Shakespeare's characteristic style, how the gap should be filled. This is what it means to trace the trajectory of the Spirit.[7]

While this illustrates very well the task of the church generally, the way forward on gender is even more clear-cut. So try this. Imagine that some children have been invited to compete on a TV game show. In the studio, they are asked to listen carefully to a series of numbers the host will announce. The challenge before them, they are told, is to tell which number ought to come next. The first person able to do so will win. So the announcer slowly intones: "Two, four, six, eight . . . ," and waits. At once an elementary-school girl blurts out "Ten!"

Was this a purely subjective notion? Not at all! She discerned the emerging pattern and was able to draw conclusions from it. True, the announcer had not actually *said* the number ten yet. But ten was definitely what everything had been leading to. It was, in fact, the one and only right answer. Discerning the trajectory of the Spirit is a lot like this. It requires insight to know where the Spirit is headed. But the process of arriving at the right answer is actually a disciplined rather than subjective one. More than anything else, it requires paying attention to what has happened so far.

A Challenge to Static Understandings

Nevertheless, a redemptive movement hermeneutic does challenge a conventional static understanding of Scripture's divine authority. It raises the suggestion that the authors of Scripture themselves may have been at the time of writing still in process of theological growth and formation. Many evangelicals assume that through the inspiration and superintendence of the Holy Spirit the authors of Scripture always wrote perfectly polished and "finished" truth statements. There is no allowance for the possibility that inspired writing, like normal writing, could be a means by which authors thought themselves clear on an issue.

It is important to explain that a redemptive movement hermeneutic does not imply that Scripture is ever wrong. It is still viewed as entirely right, but right in a way that perhaps some of us did not fully appreciate before. This hermeneutic also contains a salutary reminder that we must prioritize the directional flow of Scripture over questionable inferences from eclectic texts. "We must not be limited to a mere enactment of the text's isolated words. It is our sacred calling to champion its spirit."[8] We are most intent on hearing the living Word, "which moves forth from its dynamic biblical matrix to ever-new chapters of expression in the church."[9]

A progressive hermeneutic pays more attention to signs of shifting and movement within the great continuum of salvation history, and is not alarmed by growth within even the New Testament itself. In practice the church has already embraced this hermeneutical principle in its acknowledgment that slavery was sanctioned in the New Testament even while the seeds of its eventual overthrow were sown in the same pages. At the same time, evangelicals can be assured that this approach will not lead us down any "slippery slope" to approving all sorts of immoral behavior. One of the telltale proofs that something is wrong is that it is *consistently* denounced in Scripture. If Scripture doesn't budge on an issue, we shouldn't either.

We cannot tell how much of the full gospel vision for gender relations was consistently grasped by the different New Testament writers, or how deeply each one chose to embrace this vision in his attitudes, priorities, leadership decisions, and personal behavior. It is not our place to speculate on the private mind-set of the biblical writers. But if these writers were permitted, as they evidently were, to retain certain limitations of understanding without that impairing their ability to compose infallible Scripture, they may have labored with less than fully informed understandings of other issues as well. Biblical authors did not have to be perfect in every way to qualify as reliable instruments of divine inspiration.

We should not dismiss or condemn the redemptive movement hermeneutic as incompatible with the church's historically high view of Scripture. It contains much promise for a breakthrough in the standing impasse on these important interpretive issues. The case for gender egalitarianism can best be made by engaging in these three tasks of biblical interpretation: clarifying meaning, restricting applications, and discerning movement. Some things the Bible says about gender are normative and merely need to be clarified. Other things the Bible says about gender are contextual and ought to be treated in that restricted way. Still other things the Bible says concerning gender ought to be understood as still-partial expressions of the full implications of the gospel.

The debate over gender continues to be vigorous in the Christian community. At times our heads swim in the mass of exegetical arguments for and against the competing positions. At certain moments the debate seems like a war of attrition waged by scribes. Even the most determined student of the issues can get bogged down and bewildered by it all. There comes a point at which it is necessary to draw back for a moment from the micro-level of specific arguments—and to pull up for an aerial shot of the entire landscape. Sometimes it is helpful to be offered a vision, if only a modest sketch of one. It is with such an offering in mind that you are now invited, like an alert football receiver watching the arc of a long pass from the quarterback, to discern the trajectory of the Spirit.

chapter summary

Gender is a front-burner issue today, and Christians properly look to Scripture for guidance on the matter. As we study the Bible, we need to discern the direction the Spirit is moving as he progressively unfolds God's will. It is important to understand what the Bible *says*; it is equally important to recognize where the Bible is *headed*. The Holy Spirit is nudging the people of God today toward a fuller embrace of the gospel vision of gender equality, freedom, and mutuality. The Spirit is leading us on a long journey home to the original Garden way of doing life. And keeping in step with the Spirit requires, as we shall see, letting go of hierarchical paradigms for male-female relationships.

Questions for Individual or Group Reflection

1. Explain the three cornerstones of the gospel vision for gender relations. Which of these is most important to you personally, and why?

2. How would you define "complementarian" and "egalitarian"? What is the central issue dividing the complementarian and egalitarian sides in the current evangelical debate over gender?

3. Identify the three essential tasks of Bible interpretation. Try to give an example of each.

4. What is the basic problem with a "static" approach to interpreting the Bible?

5. How can we safeguard the "progressive movement" approach to Bible interpretation against cynical people using it to promote whatever they *want* the Bible to say?

CHAPTER 2

God Before All Things

a TRINITARIAN feLLOwSHIP of DIVINE LOVE

Archie and his daughter Abigail had always been close. Out on the farm, he had taught her how to operate his big John Deere tractor years before she was old enough for her driver's license. He'd had an expensive CD player installed in the cab, just so she could listen to her Shania Twain and Kenny Chesney music. Many a time during calving season she'd stayed up with him all night to help distressed cows deliver wobbly calves in the glare of his Ford truck's headlights. "Abigail means 'father's delight,'" Archie used to tell people in his half embarrassed, half proud way. She was the apple of his eye.

They had taken Abigail all her growing-up years to a church that prided itself in being solidly biblical. Both Archie and his wife were devout Christians, and it was killing them to see Abby drift away from the faith as she grew older. The church's treatment of women had been an issue for her since her first year at university. Thereafter things had devolved slowly, as far as Archie could tell, but he was also aware of some notable milestones along the way. For example, there was the time some well-meaning church ladies had advised her not to pursue a graduate degree because it might make her too intimidating, and ultimately less appealing, to eligible Christian men. That had gotten her steaming.

Then there was a fateful communion service a few years back, when, as usual, the crackers and grape juice were handed down the pews by the deacons—all men, of course, for that was church policy.

Staring straight ahead, with arms crossed, Abby had let the tinny silver trays pass her by. On the way out, however, she had unloaded on the poor greeter at the door: "Did it ever occur to you that it was Mary—a *woman*—who nurtured Jesus Christ in her own body, birthed him herself, and then gave him to the world to be their Savior?" The bewildered man was speechless as she continued, almost shouting now: "Does it not strike you as *ironic* that now in this church, women are considered unfit to pray over, and unsuited even to distribute, *symbols* of that same Savior's body and blood? What's *wrong* with you people?"

She started her car and screeched out of the gravel parking lot. She never went back. The *coup de grace* came a few months later, when her Christian boyfriend advised her that if they ever got married she would need to enthusiastically acknowledge his loving headship. "Are you suggesting that I should plan to *submit* to you just because you're a man?" she had asked, incredulously.

"I'm not suggesting anything. I'm *telling* you," he had replied. Well, that was the end of that. Abby headed off into her own wide open spaces. Archie tries to stay in touch. There was pain on his face as he turned and said, "I just don't understand it. I think those feminists at the university must have gotten to her. Why is it such a put-down on women to expect them to submit to men?"

"The way I look at it," he said—more to himself than to me, really—and I knew he was trying to process things through the filter of his Christian worldview, "Jesus was God, right?"

"Absolutely," I responded. "He was fully divine."

"OK. But didn't Jesus say to his heavenly Father, 'Not my will, but yours be done,' and lots of other submissive stuff like that?"

Again I readily agreed that it was so. "Well then," Archie continued, "if Jesus was equal to the Father, but could still be subordinate to him, why is it so inappropriate or demeaning to ask women to submit to men? I mean, if Jesus could handle submission, why can't women today?" From the look on his face I could tell he considered the logic of his argument virtually airtight.

Archie had just laid out the ultimate celebrity endorsement of hierarchical gender relations. He was absolutely sincere, and I respected my friend, even though I disagreed with him. "Archie," I replied, "I commend you for factoring God into this. I agree with you that God's nature and actions are the ultimate benchmark for what is right and proper. And the way the persons of the Trinity interact just might provide the example we need for how men and women ought to relate to one another.

"But I think there's a flaw in your line of reasoning, and in the end it looms pretty large. It seems to me you've overlooked the fact that the Son was subordinate to the Father *while he was human*—and humans, of course, should always defer to God. But aside from that brief time when the Son lived on earth as one of us, there's never been (and in my opinion never will be) any need for a boss in the Trinity."

"What are you saying?" Archie rejoined with a faint hint of alarm. "You better explain yourself." And so, while he listened patiently and the cows ruminated in the corral next to us, I shared with him what I understood of God. If you are not interested in my response to Archie's question, feel free to skip ahead to the next chapter. But if you're curious, hang in there. What I said to Archie went something like this.

In the Beginning God

Our imaginations fail us when we try to peer into the mystery of what it was like prior to anything familiar—prior to the creation of all things. The veil was not completely lifted, it seems, even for the inspired writer of the biblical account of creation, who was compelled finally to describe the Eternally Prior in these words, as we have it in the dignified prose of the King James Version: "And the earth was without form, and void; and darkness was upon the face of the deep" (Gen. 1:2).

But this is not the whole story. For in the midst of this infinite nothingness and absolutely dark silence a presence brooded—a pulsating, living reality, the great I Am, the God who was and is and ever shall be. The eternal one, inexplicable in origin, had always been present. God alone was there, and because of God's presence the emptiness was actually full of spiritual glory. The darkness radiated with spiritual light. On an ethereal frequency the silence echoed the fulsome chords of exultation and delight. There was no need to populate the wasted space with stuff, to furnish the barren rooms of nothingness with filler. God was all and in all, magnificent in glory, and more than sufficient to justify the extravagance.

But there is more. This God was far more than a dynamic force. He was well beyond the sum of the laws governing and guiding the universe. He was a personal God. Certainly he was not a "person" in the sense that he was (as the ancient Greeks, and many others, idolized him) a supersized human being. He was altogether beyond our conceptual categories. But he was, and forever remains, a personal being. He is personal in the sense that he is not an "it." He is a subject, not an object. He is conscious, alive, and free. He interacts with, and responds to, other personal beings. He can and does express himself—he communicates. And he delights in relationship. This is the Christian vision of God. The Old and New Testaments assure us that God really is this way. So personhood lies at the very heart and core of the universe—the ultimate reality is not material but personal.

Our wonder grows as we investigate further. For the personal God who dwelt in solitary majesty was actually not alone, after all. True, there was nothing in all eternity that was not God. But the startling revelation is that there was *within* the being of this one-and-only God himself a mysterious plurality—a diversity of being. God was perfectly One (the monotheistic religious traditions have been emphatically right about that), but his oneness consisted of a unity in diversity. This is a baffling truth which Christianity's two cousin religions in the West, Judaism and Islam, have been unable or unwilling to acknowledge. In fairness, it is a truth-claim that seems almost too much for reasonable people anywhere to embrace.

Yet the deeper-reaching theologians of the orthodox Christian tradition have understood that God is a unity of three distinct persons in "a trinitarian fellowship of holy love."[1] The Father, the Son, and the Holy Spirit—these three—are eternally together in an interactive community of being. Love is the Trinity's interior atmosphere. And, as C. S. Lewis explained, this "living, dynamic activity of love has been going on in God forever and has created everything else."[2]

It is worth noting that God's signature style of relating is one free of domineering behavior and intimidation. Clearly God appreciates the fact that heavy-handed control tactics are alien to, and destructive of, the best experiences of love and the deepest relationships of friendship. Everything about God's ways of relating to humans through the centuries would bear this out. But before all that, this style of relating was already a reality in the inner life of the triune God. The choices of "Father" and "Son" as names for two of the persons of the Godhead were never meant to imply that the Father is older, more important, or deserving of more respect, than the Son. Rather, the language of Father and Son was chosen by God to convey the idea of familial-like intimacy of relationship—the closest, if still imperfect, analogy with which to bridge from the nature of the transcendent God to the realm of our everyday human experience.

In his classic *The Knowledge of the Holy*, A. W. Tozer notes that "what comes into our minds when we think about God is the most important thing about us."[3] This is absolutely true. There is an imitative principle operating in all religions, and this principle simply means that over time a sincere worshiper (the principle only works in the case of *serious* worshipers) will inevitably become more and more like that which he or she adores. There is, in other words, an involuntary correlation between the perceived profile of a deity and the general characteristics and values of the adherents to that religion. So it is important, therefore, that we get *true* things established in our minds when we think about God. Among other things, we need to know whether the Trinity is hierarchical or not.

A Trinity of Equals

Not long ago I visited Istanbul, Turkey, and stood beneath the gargantuan dome of Hagia Sophia, which was Christendom's greatest church for a thousand years. I recalled that in this very place, Constantinople, and in nearby communities like Nicea and Chalcedon, some of the finest intellects of history concentrated their minds on the mystery of God's nature. Eventually, those Christians had to admit that they would never be able to get their heads *completely* around

God. From the perspective of spirituality, that was probably a healthy realization, for it encouraged them to show God even greater reverence and worship. Nevertheless, they did not believe God had left them completely in the dark. As they reflected together on biblical revelation, they gradually reached consensus on a number of points. But it took the church a long time—centuries, in fact—to think itself clear on the Trinity.

From the vantage point of the twenty-first century, it is a bit surprising to discover how widely the church's early speculations on the Trinity initially ranged. Church fathers who otherwise are greatly venerated to this day often expressed some rather startling and conflicting opinions about the triune God.[4] We should be charitable toward these theological pioneers. They were fallible people like we are, and intellectually they were venturing to go where no one had gone before.

Early on, for example, some church leaders and theologians speculated that the Son and the Spirit, the so-called second and third persons of the Trinity, were less eternal than the Father. The Son and Spirit had come along later than the Father, so to speak, and were therefore slightly inferior in their essential being (or, as it is sometimes expressed, they were *ontologically* inferior to the Father). More than anything else it appears to have been the language of John the evangelist about the Father "begetting" the Son (John 1:14 KJV) and the Spirit "proceeding" from the Father (John 15:26 KJV) that got them off track. They took John's imagery of procreation literally rather than analogically. That was a mistake.

Thanks in no small part to the heroic efforts of Athanasius, a consensus emerged that the three persons of the Trinity are ontologically equal. This was much more than a mere academic matter for Athanasius. He was convinced that the adequacy and effectiveness of Christ's saving work depended on the unqualified divinity of the Son, and so he pressed the issue for years. More than once he was demoted and banished for his convictions, and for a while he was little more than a lone voice crying in the wilderness. In time, however, the Christian community was won over to his interpretation and believed that its doctrinal consensus reflected the guidance of the Spirit of God.

Eventually these truths were enshrined in the Nicene Creed (325 AD), and have ever since been associated with mainstream Christian orthodoxy. The Son of God is confessed to be "God from God . . . true God from true God . . . begotten, not made." And further, it boldly declared that Christ is "of one substance with the Father." The idea was that the Son cannot be more God than he is: he was and remains as God as God can be. Later, in an expanded version of this same creed, known as the Nicene-Constantinopolitan Creed (381 AD), the point was added that the Holy Spirit, "the Lord and giver of life," is to be worshiped and glorified with the Father and Son. To sum matters up, the church declared that there are no graded levels of God-ness in the Trinity.

Moreover, the biblical language concerning the begetting of the Son (Acts 13:33) was understood to refer to an *eternal* begetting, so that no one should ever think that there was a time when the Son did not already coexist with the Father. Likewise the apostle John's language of the Spirit's proceeding from the Father (John 15:26) was understood as an *eternal* procession, so that no one should ever imagine a moment when the Spirit had not yet proceeded forth from the Father. There is no level of supreme God-ness to which the Son and Spirit do not fully attain alongside the Father.

Is God the Father in Charge?

But a subtler theological issue was not so easily resolved. This was whether the three equal-in-essence persons of the Trinity might possibly still relate to one another according to the dynamics of authority and subordination. In other words, one of the questions that Christians pondered was how they should understand the "structure" of the Trinity. Did the three persons of the Trinity relate to one another in a particular order? Was the primacy of one person necessary to united action and the harmonious administration of their relationships? Such questions would seem impossible to answer, except that God has graciously revealed things about himself that he intends us to consider and take seriously. I am sure you can see how important practical matters related to gender hinge on our conclusions about God.

Through the years quite a few sincere Christians have assumed that the social structure of the Trinity is hierarchical. For them, the reality of God can be represented geometrically by a triangle with the Father at the top. The early church father Tertullian (160–225 AD) got Christians started down this road when he suggested that while Christ was equal in *nature* to the Father, he was second in *position* within the Trinity.[5] A lot of classic Christian art, which once served as visual pedagogy for the illiterate, reinforced this kind of thinking. It has depicted the Father as a powerful figure, far up in the clouds and clearly in charge, while the Son is portrayed as operating submissively in parts lower down. During our visits to Italian art museums this past year, my daughter Claire, an art history major, drew my attention to a recurring artistic depiction of the Trinity as three separate beings posing, so to speak, for a family photo. At the center is the Son on a heavy cross. Behind and above him, with arms extended in undergirding support, is the larger, more powerful Father. The Holy Spirit hovers in the foreground as a small, relatively inconsequential dove. You can find such Trinity portraiture all over Italy and elsewhere—even on postcards. It is unfortunate, because the visual differentials in size have been so seriously misleading.

To those who took the "father and son" imagery of biblical revelation *literally*, this seemed reasonable enough. The Ten Commandments insist that children should obey their parents (Ex. 20:12). It made sense that the Son of God should be a good example of the submission God expected children to show toward their earthly parents. Surely God would not hold human beings to a moral standard from which he himself was exempt. The flaw in this line of reasoning, of course, is that the "father and son" imagery is *imagery*, and should *not* be taken literally.

Something else inclined some Christians to view the Trinity as a hierarchy. Most of the social organizations (including marriage and family life) with which the early Christians were familiar worked this way. In each of these cases someone was the boss. It was assumed that someone always had to be in charge, or the social organization would quickly degenerate into anarchy and chaos.

There was yet another factor that predisposed them to interpret Trinitarian life hierarchically. That was the record in the New Testament of how Jesus, the incarnate Son of God, related to his heavenly Father. Some biblical statements give the impression that saving initiatives originated with the Father, and that the Son then cooperated with the Father's desires. For example, John 3:16 says that God (and God the Father appears to be in view) so loved the world that he gave his only Son. Subsequently, the Son's passion was to do the Father's will and accomplish the work assigned to him (John 4:34), even if his submission to the Father's will involved an agonizing struggle. According to this view of things, the Son's relationship to the Father can be summed up in Christ's immortal prayer in the garden of Gethsemane: "Not my will, but yours be done" (Luke 22:42).

If these dynamics truly reflect the way the Father and the Son relate, we are talking about the functional subordination of the Son. According to this view, the Father has a certain primacy of stature in the Trinity, and because of this is entitled to decide what should be done when issues come up. For their parts, the Son and the Spirit are expected to go along with what the Father decides and decrees. All three persons are equal in essential nature, but the Father is, so to speak, in charge.

The Trinity Is Not a Pyramid

The majority of Christians, however, have interpreted the Son's relationship to the Father's will differently than this. For one thing, the majority have never regarded Jesus Christ as a reluctant accomplice to the Father's plans. They have steadfastly refused to consider Christ's self-sacrificial actions as motivated chiefly by a sense of loyal duty to his heavenly Father's will. Rather, the consensus among Christians has been that Christ was motivated in large part by his own compassion for lost people. God's love for the world is not a love more intensely present in the Father than in the Son.

It is an assault on the unity of the triune God to suggest that without the Father's strong initiative and persistence, the Son might have declined to participate in, or follow through on, the plan of redemption.

It suggests multiple divine hearts struggling against one another. The creeds of the church have established that the will of God is ultimately one unified will, not a trio of dissonant volition centers one might expect if God were three gods in a consortium. While that view of things might be compatible with pagan notions of multiple gods of unequal virtue, it can never be reconciled with the revealed truth that God is irreducibly and perfectly one in nature and will.

But how should we understand the interior life of the Trinity in *eternity*? If dynamics of unequal authority and submission persist between the persons of the Trinity, we are talking about the *eternal* functional subordination of the Son to the Father. Such a view of things has been present in Christianity through the centuries, but (perhaps surprisingly, given how much hierarchical assumptions pervaded the consciousness) it has never been dominant in the theology of Western Christianity. Indeed, the majority position from the early centuries onward has been to set aside hierarchy and subordination in favor of a vision of harmonious mutuality in the interior life of God.[6]

Augustine's magisterial fifth-century work *On the Trinity* is, among other things, a robust defense of the complete equality (in both essence and eternal function) of the three persons of the triune God. If someone suggests that the Father is greater than the Son in any way whatsoever, Augustine warned, it is because they have mistakenly transferred "those things which are said of Jesus Christ according to the flesh, to that substance of His which was eternal before the incarnation, and is eternal." Here is the critical distinction between the eternal Trinity and the temporary manifestation of the Trinity in human history. Augustine set this out as a basic interpretative principle: every biblical reference to the Son being lesser or below the Father (that is, every indication of functional subordination) pertains only to the Son's incarnate, "servant" form (Phil. 2:7).[7]

By the early sixth century, the Athanasian Creed had become a highly regarded expression of the emergent Christian consensus on the Trinity. It was totally consistent with the earlier high Christology of Athanasius (and perhaps for that reason bears his name), and at the same time reflected subsequent Augustinian insights on the Trinity.

Most of it was devoted to affirming the full and unqualified equality of the Godhead. Toward the end, attention briefly turns to whether the Son and the Father relate to one another according to a hierarchical arrangement. Here, significantly, the Athanasian Creed describes the Son as "equal to the Father in respect of his divinity, less than (Latin, *minor*) the Father in respect of his humanity."[8] This plainly echoes the earlier view of Augustine—namely, that every biblical instance of hierarchical relationship between the persons of the Trinity is due entirely and exclusively to the Son taking on our humanity. Thus all authority and subordination language in the New Testament reflects the differential between God and humanity rather than anything intrinsic or essential to the Godhead itself.

The Protestant Reformers espoused the same nonhierarchical vision of the eternal Trinity, and in turn these Reformers' views were enshrined in various Protestant confessions of faith. The Second Helvetic Confession (1566), for example, considered it a blasphemy to teach that any person of the Trinity is "subservient or subordinate" to another.[9] Thereafter, the dubious doctrine of the eternal subordination (or subservience) of the Son remained undersubscribed in the mainstream of Protestant theology, and has fortunately stayed the minority view in Western Christianity.

Of course, by themselves these historical facts do not make the case for eternal mutuality within the Trinity a conclusive one for evangelicals. This is because evangelicals do not attach final authority to any merely human tradition. But the fact that throughout history Christians have generally declined to endorse eternal functional subordination ought at least to give us pause, and prompt us to inquire into the reasons why this has been so.

Debunking the Fallacy of a Split-Level Trinity

For weeks our seminary class had been plowing its way through Christology—the study of Jesus Christ. We were studying those instances in the New Testament in which Jesus was dependent upon, and submissive to, God the Father. I had suggested that it makes most sense to see this earthly hierarchical relationship between the Father and the

Son as occasioned entirely by Christ's adoption of our humanity and its associated limitations. This explanation had been introduced into the Christian tradition by Augustine himself 1,700 years ago. As Philippians 2 explains, the eternal Son voluntarily humbled himself in order to become one with us, yet without ever becoming less than fully God in the process. As part of his decision to fully identify with humanity, the Son chose to hide his true glory and to relinquish his right to independently exercise his divine powers and prerogatives.[10]

By entering human existence as one of us, the Son was able to live as an example of how humanity restored to the image of God ought to live in relation to the Father. For a brief time, the Son lived on earth under the limitations we experience, and he looked to the Father (just as we must) for needed guidance, power, and even courage at the end. Significantly, this was only a temporary arrangement. Once his mission on earth was accomplished, the earlier dynamics of perfect equality between the persons of the Trinity resumed.

Gloria, one of the class participants, caught up with me in the hallway afterward. "Got a minute?" she asked.

"Got coffee?" I countered with a smile. Gloria is a navy commander who oversees all the navy hospitals and medical facilities in our region of the United States. She's sharp and exudes leadership presence. In the next few years she's hoping to transition into a second career in vocational ministry.

Gloria got to her point as soon as we found seats. "I'm intrigued by what we discussed in class today about the Son's equality with the Father. I guess I just need to make double-sure that what you're saying is *biblical*. Would you mind walking me through it just one more time?"

"Not at all," I replied. "I think it is very important to ask the question of biblical faithfulness, Gloria. I also think the best place to start is the Philippians 2:6–11 passage that came up earlier today. It's particularly helpful because it begins by indicating that in eternity the Son enjoyed *equality* with the Father (v. 6). Later, in order to become human and save us, he elected not to keep a tight grip on it. Instead, he lovingly let it go.

"But exactly which *aspect* of equality with the Father did he give up? Could it have been his equality of nature and being with the Father?"

"Impossible," Gloria declared without hesitation. "If that were the case, it would have amounted to a loss of divinity. He would not have been fully God anymore. He would have become an *ex*-God, a *former* deity, and a merely human Messiah. That simply can't be the answer we're looking for."

"I agree wholeheartedly," I said. "But think about it. The only other possibility is that he relinquished his *functional* equality with the Father. If his essential nature remained intact, it must have been his equality of glory, position, and function that he temporarily surrendered. Philippians 2 goes on to say that he took the form of a *servant* (v. 7), which suggests that Christ's original equality with God the Father was the exact opposite of being a servant to anyone."

"That makes sense," said Gloria. "And it fits nicely with something else I noticed. Philippians does not say the Son *was* humbled—rather, it says he humbled *himself* (v. 8). In other words, it was *his* decision. As someone has put it, 'Christ did not take upon himself the task of world redemption because he was number two in the Trinity and the boss told him to do so.'"[11]

"Exactly," I replied. "So do you see where this now logically leads us?"

"I believe I do," said Gloria. "The Son could only give up what he already possessed. Temporarily surrendering his right to function as the Father's perfect equal means that up until then he *did* function as the Father's equal, rather than under him or in subordination to him. The Son could give up role parity in the Trinity only because he had it in the first place.

"The military is pretty top-down, you know, so it's all a paradigm shift for me," Gloria said, checking her watch and rising to leave, "but I think I'm starting to see it. The eternal relationship between Father and Son precludes permanent subordination and any notions of a split-level Trinity."

All I could say was Amen.

Christ Temporarily Subordinate as a Human

But, someone may persist, what should we make of Jesus' statement, recorded in John 14:28, that "the Father is greater than I"? By the end of the first five centuries, as we noted earlier, the Christian community had achieved a solid consensus that the Father was not greater than the Son in substance or essential nature. That is what the creedal term *homoousios* (meaning that Christ was of *the same essence* as the Father) was intended to establish beyond equivocation. But could this statement possibly mean that the Son is at the same time eternally subordinate to the Father in *function*? Could the Son, in other words, be equal in essence to the Father, but at the same time eternally subordinate in role? Could both be simultaneously true?

Obviously the Son was functionally subordinate to the Father during his saving sojourn on earth. There was an undeniable authority differential in the way they related to one another. Nonetheless, John Calvin spoke for mainstream Christian interpretation (and in accord with Augustine's outlook centuries before) when he insisted that the surpassing greatness of the Father, to which John 14:28 refers, is only a temporary and temporal differential. It refers only to the relative brightness of the Father's heavenly splendor as it contrasts to the Son's glory, which was briefly veiled by the Son's taking on of ordinary humanity.[12] In general, theologians since Augustine have insisted that "all texts which speak of the Son's subordination refer exclusively to his earthly ministry."[13]

A similar interpretation properly applies to Scripture passages which describe the eternal future, and *appear* to give the Father priority over the Son even there. For example, the Scriptures say that someday Christ will hand over the kingdom to God the Father (1 Cor. 15:24), and "the Son himself will be made subject to him who put everything under him, so that *God* may be all in all" (1 Cor. 15:28, my emphasis). Once again it is wisest to interpret these passages along the lines Calvin commended. According to Calvin, the apostle Paul wanted to be clear that the exaltation of Christ will respect only one ceiling—it will not catapult him up into a level *above* the existing God of the universe.

These statements in 1 Corinthians anticipate a day when the saving work of Christ will be complete, and everything that needs to be done will have been done. At that point, the distinctions of roles in historic redemption (that is, the so-called "economic roles") between the persons of the Trinity, including the temporary subordination of the Son as a fellow earthling with us, will become superfluous. By then, God's objectives will have been fully achieved. The useful *ad hoc* arrangement that involved the historic subordination of the Son to the Father will be permanently dismantled, and followed by a restoration of the unified radiance of the eternally triune God. As it was in the beginning, so it will be ever thereafter, world without end.

The New Testament's depictions of Christ at the right hand of God the Father on high (Luke 22:69; Acts 2:33; Col. 3:1) should be interpreted in the same way. Taken in the flow of their respective settings, these descriptions of Christ were clearly intended to convey the unparalleled height of Christ's triumph and exaltation. To be situated at the right hand of God meant that the resurrected Christ now has divine power and cosmic authority. Given the idiomatic sense of the "right hand," the image may also have been intended to convey the idea that Christ is the instrument or means by which the will of the triune God is administered in the world. All things are thereby *through* Christ.

It is ironic that this imagery of Christ's profound exaltation should ever be interpreted as a basis for diminishing his coequal status in the Godhead. But it certainly has been. As one prominent complementarian reads this text, "Jesus is at the right hand, but God the Father is still on the throne."[14] But surely the point being made through this imagery is that Christ is actually reseated with God the Father, not that he has been placed on some auxiliary seating adjacent to the real center of power. This way of imaging Christ in the heavenly realms was the inspired author's way of expressing Christ's full authority, without denying the distinction of persons within the Trinity. In Revelation 22:1, the apostle John describes the restoration of Eden's purity and peace, and the water of life "flowing from the throne of God and of the Lamb." Here the throne is singular, and there is *no distinction* made between the Father and the Son when it comes to who occupies it.

Bowman's Garage

I have heard people suggest that not even the persons of the Trinity can function without a designated boss. It is an interesting claim, and one I reflected on while getting my car repaired at my regular spot— Bowman's Garage off El Cajon Boulevard. The greasy little office, noticeably lacking Martha Stewart touches, has its own unpretentious charm. It was a slow day, and I learned from the guys sitting around on break that when the original owner, Mr. Bowman, passed away, two of his mechanics, Bill and Roberto, stepped up and bought the place.

And so for the past twenty-five years, these two men, my mechanics—genial, laconic, and honest—have been operating the business as a partnership. Neither of them is boss, and yet they seem to be managing just fine. I couldn't help but think: if the owners of an auto and transmission repair shop in southern California can operate cheerfully and efficiently, year after year, without any hierarchical structure of leadership, it seems a curious thing to doubt whether the infinite God of the universe is capable of doing the same.

Complete Mutuality Just Makes Sense

The majority Christian theological tradition has viewed the Trinity as a community of persons equal in being, rank, and function. This wide stream begins with magisterial figures like Athanasius, Augustine, and Aquinas, and continues through B. B. Warfield of Old Princeton to such credible evangelical theologians today as Millard Erickson, who writes of the three persons of the Trinity:

> Each is essential to the life of the others, and to the life of the Trinity. They are bound to one another in love, *agape* love, which therefore unites them in the closest and most intimate of relationships. This unselfish, *agape* love makes each more concerned for the other than for himself. There is therefore a mutual submission of each to each of the others and a mutual glorifying of one another. There is complete equality of the three.[15]

While the staying power of a doctrine should carry weight with us in sorting out our convictions about the Trinity, tradition is not by itself a definitive test of truth. The sixteenth-century Protestant Reformers had a Latin motto, *semper reformata* (literally, always reforming), which meant that imperfect theological traditions need perpetual reformation as the truth of God's Word comes into ever clearer focus. Those who believe this way will never treat a traditional understanding as final, simply because it carries venerable credentials. Ultimately, we must also consider theological issues directly and personally, and assess which view is most in accord with the true intent of Scripture.

Historically, one consideration has proven especially decisive in leading Christians to believe that the Trinity is truly a nonhierarchical community of mutual love. It is an inference from the fact that the substance, or essence, of God is shared equally by the three persons of the Godhead, and that the fullness of the Deity dwells in each one. All this being so, the classic reasoning goes, it is ultimately nonsensical to think that one member of the Trinity would eternally stand in a relationship of primacy or authority over another person of the Trinity when all possess an equal and complete God-quality. It would be as though the God-quality of one member of the Godhead was somehow superior to the God-quality of the other, or that the skill-set of one member was superior to the range of competencies of another. No matter how you tried to explain it, God would end up being inferior to God! Biblical references to distinct activities of persons of the Trinity in eternity always indicate free and untiered *arrangements*, rather than any vertical command structure, within God.

Consider this as well. Hierarchies *are* appropriate whenever there are genuine differentials in ability. Patients should listen to their doctors, because their doctors went to medical school and see problems like theirs all the time. Some people are qualified to fly commercial airplanes, and others should be content to travel as their passengers. The skies are safer when these distinctions are strictly observed! Likewise, military officers are trained and qualified to command and, because of this, more junior personnel should normally follow their orders. These are all legitimate distinctions, and the world in general runs better because of them. Likewise, the difference between God and humanity is one that warrants a distinction in functional authority and roles.

Regrettably, vertical power structures within humanity are often advocated by the strong because they wish to exert control over society's weaker members. Still, such abuses do not invalidate hierarchical arrangements as long as they are warranted, appropriately restrained, and morally legitimate.

At the same time we should challenge hierarchical structures based on an illegitimate distinction between those who are allowed to rule and those who must obey. We have no problem with the military distinction between a colonel and a sergeant, for example, unless the assignment of these ranks is based on ethnicity. In such a case, one person might be eligible to become a general because of skin color, while another might be denied that opportunity for the same reason. We would consider such a hierarchical system racist and unjust.

There is a direct application here to our view of God (and God-like gender relations). On what grounds could a Trinitarian hierarchy conceivably be established, let alone be necessary? If each person of the Trinity is equal to the others in infinite honor, holiness, wisdom, and love, how could the smallest difference of opinion, or the least breach of perfect unity, possibly develop among the members? Where there is a community without the faintest trace of inferiority, sin, ignorance, or selfishness among the members, what conceivable need would there be for a hierarchical ordering of persons and wills? In such a context, surely hierarchy would be completely superfluous.

Athanasius was convinced that any privileging of the Father over the Son, however minor or subtle, would inevitably lead to a diminishing of the Son's claim to full divinity. Yet "in Christ all the fullness of the Deity lives in bodily form" (Col. 2:9), Athanasius insisted, and on the continued affirmation of this unqualified truth hinged the future of Christianity itself. Church history has vindicated Athanasius. Anything less has inevitably led to diminishing Christ himself. And anything less will certainly be a defective and inferior model for what God desires for women and men as well.

Back on the farm, my friend had been very patient as I shared all this from my heart. "Well, Archie," I asked as I wrapped up my monologue, "what do you think? Did I make my case?"

He slowly turned toward me. Cautiously he drawled, in the language of the King James Version he'd memorized as a child, "Almost thou persuadest me" (Acts 26:28). We laughed together. Just from the way Archie said it, though, I felt encouraged. He was the kind of person who would mull it all over very carefully. After a moment, he added quietly: "If it turns out you're right, I certainly plan to tell Abby. It might just be the breakthrough we've been looking for."

Actually, that was just the beginning of the good news. And that's what the rest of this book is all about. The story continues in the next chapter with the creation of human beings.

chapter summary

In the beginning there was God, a three-person fellowship of holy love, whose inner atmosphere was perfect mutuality. God celebrated this diversity of persons without fear of complication or chaos, for the eternal harmony of Father, Son, and Holy Spirit required neither control, unequal submission, nor forced uniformity. God had no need for vertical power structures within himself. The inner atmosphere of the triune God was perfect love among equals (John 17:24–26)—free and reciprocal self-giving of each for the other. We have been created and called to be like God, which includes imitating the way the persons of the Trinity eternally relate to one another. This vision of God is where our own transformation must begin.

Questions for Individual or Group Reflection

1. Why is the nature of the Trinity relevant to the topic of male-female relationships?

2. Does every relationship require that one person be the leader? When is hierarchy in a relationship appropriate?

3. Why does it matter whether or not the Son is eternally subordinate to the Father?

4. What should we make of those biblical texts in which Jesus submitted to his Father's will and claimed that the Father was greater than he?

5. What important insight does the Athanasian Creed contain concerning Christ's relationship to the Father?

CHapter 3

Created to Be Like God

maLe aND femaLe IN ReLatIONSHIP

God was before all things—glorious and perfectly self-sufficient. For all eternity past there was absolutely nothing else on the horizon. What happened next had no precedent. It could not possibly have been anticipated. But it *did* happen, and that is the wonder of it. In the midst of this serene nothingness, somewhere out in the darkness, suddenly and without warning there was a mighty release of power and light. A force of unimaginable magnitude exploded in every direction at once, roiling and tumbling out from its blinding center.

The intensity of the heat and the awesome energy was overwhelming. A vast array of massive objects appeared out of nowhere, projectiles of astonishing number, density, and speed. They hurtled out into the dark unknown with a stampeding, trampling fervor, like a mighty, rushing wind, with such an incredible surge of momentum that they would not begin to cool or slow their screaming vectors for countless years to come. The astronomers at the Hubble space telescope are still trying to figure out exactly what happened.

Let There Be Light!

Creation had begun. And it was the work of the triune God, who detonated it all by a simple and majestic order: *Let there be light!* Reality was altered forever. For the first time there was time, and something that was not God. From now on, reality would consist of God *and* that which was not God. Though magnificent and wondrous, and worthy of its creator, that which was brought into being was finite. It did not share in God's infinite attributes. But it did mirror something of its creator's character. For those with eyes to see, it was engraved with his signature and marked by his footprints. The heavens declared the glory of God.

The real event—the historical fact—of divine creation is beautifully narrated in poetic form in the first chapter of Genesis, the book of beginnings. It is an inspired and beautiful depiction of God's originating work, from the perspective of a reverent earth-dweller looking all around, and up, with amazement. God's wisdom and sensitivity are portrayed, in concert with his power, as he crafts a fragile ecosystem designed to sustain an extravagant diversity of life forms. We are left to wonder at the significance of the reported method of creation, but certainly John Calvin was on the mark when he suggested that "we ought in the very order of things diligently to contemplate God's fatherly love toward mankind, in that he did not create Adam until he had lavished upon the universe all manner of good things."[1] Everything so far has been prelude. We're poised and ready for the main event.

Creatures Like God

Finally, as Calvin's remark anticipates, we reach the zenith—the high point—of the creation process. Humanity steps on stage. God said: "Let us make human beings in our image, in our likeness" (Gen. 1:26 TNIV). And so, we are told, it came to pass: "God created human beings in his own image, in the image of God he created them; male and female he created them" (v. 27 TNIV). Like all the other creatures, these first human beings were finite. They were not God. But there was an important distinction introduced here. Unlike all the other creatures, these humans were in the image and likeness of God. The defining feature of first-ever humanity was the *imago Dei*.

A few people draw a distinction between the so-called "image" and "likeness" of God, as though these were two subtly distinct attributes of humanity. But nowhere else in Scripture is there any hint of such a distinction. The wiser approach, therefore, is to accept that the term "likeness" is here to clarify that "image" in this context means significant similarity, not exact equivalence. The word "likeness" was meant to explain that humans are *like* God, but never were, or ever will be, *identical to* God.

Humanity's essential God-likeness is the basis for human dignity and worth in the Jewish and Christian traditions. This is why human life is sacred and deserving of protection. Huston Smith reminds us of "a rabbinic saying to the effect that whenever a man or woman walks down the street he or she is preceded by an invisible choir of angels crying, 'Make way, make way! Make way for the image of God.'"[2] That is the spirit of the Christian understanding of humanity's essential worth. Christian apologist C. S. Lewis made the same point in his own inimitable way when he said: "There are no *ordinary* people. You have never talked to a mere mortal."[3] The image of God is the quality of humanity that makes evil treatment of a human being—any human, whether a spouse or a detainee—such an outrage (Gen. 9:6; James 3:9).

This truth was never meant to foster the kind of selfish human speciesism that justifies the ungodly ransacking of the planet and the cavalier annihilation of other, less powerful life forms whenever it serves the needs or convenience of the God-like species. Other balancing biblical commands, like the call to global stewardship in Genesis 2:15, make this obvious. The way forward toward planetary survival and environmental care does not lie in diminishing the dignity and worth of human beings, but in reclaiming humanity's calling to be responsible earth stewards.

Equally God-like

Neither likeness to God, nor the intrinsic personal worth that derives from it, are possessed in greater or lesser degree by one or the other of the two sexes. Male and female are equally in the image of God. Men and women are *equally* God-like. This is the bedrock foundation for any truly Christian understanding of gender. Although it was not always so, this is a truth that is, happily, only very rarely contested now among Christians.

This truth serves as a rebuke to those who claim that God is more like a man than a woman and conversely, that a man is somehow more like God than a woman can ever hope to be. Such "privileging" of the male is a crude and totally unwarranted inference from the biblical imagery of divine fatherhood (which is really about strong, protective parenthood). It reflects a near-idolatrous spin on the Scripture's own pure and spiritual understanding of God. To scale down God to humanoid proportions like this is to confuse creatures with their Creator (Rom. 1:23), which, in the apostle Paul's mind, is always spiritually fatal. We need to rigorously resist such thinking in the church today.

I vividly remember a Bible college freshman class I taught some years ago. About 180 students filled the lecture theater that fall, and I posed to them this question: "We know that in becoming human God took on a male form. But theoretically, could God have come as a woman instead?" Instantly, a fellow in the front row dramatically threw his arms apart and shouted: "Of course not! It would have been . . . uh, demeaning to God, and . . . well, blasphemous!" The room fell silent. He had gone over the line. I saw the blood drain from his face as the young man comprehended his folly in publicizing his private prejudice against women. Since then, I have often wondered how many Christians think the same way, but prudently keep their mouths shut.

God is *not* male, but a widespread misreading of the symbolic language of the Bible has led some to assume otherwise. Those who continue to indulge notions of a male God, or a God who tilts slightly toward being male-like, will be responsible for driving many female seekers away from Christ and goading them to dismiss the Christian faith as a hopelessly male-prioritizing religion. This is already happening. In the face of this trend, it is inexcusable to stubbornly perpetuate such misunderstandings of God and humanity. Genesis 1:27, with its unequivocal declaration that God created male and female in his image, trumps such pernicious silliness. Men and women are equally image-bearers of the divine.

What Is the Image?

What is it about humanity that is uniquely God-like? Or, to pose the question another way, of what does the image of God consist? As the Swiss theologian Emil Brunner insightfully observed, "The whole Christian doctrine of [humanity] hangs upon the interpretation of this expression."[4] While the implications of our interpretation will be significant, the choice is complicated, for there have been different Christian answers to this question put forward through the centuries. There are essentially four views: the *functional*, the *substantive*, the *moral*, and the *relational*. Fortunately, it is not necessary to select just one view of the image of God, and reject all the others. The concept of the image of God in humanity is "thick" enough to incorporate all four. While the substantive sense is foundational to the rest, the image of God in humanity is also functional and moral, and finds its completion in the relational.

The Functional

The *functional* view of the image of God arose from observing that the first biblical reference to the image of God is followed immediately by the so-called creation mandate, "and let them rule" (Gen. 1:26). The functional view, then, sees the image as a capacity to perform superior tasks, and assume leadership responsibilities, in creation. It sees God-likeness as being able to act like God acts. God governs the universe, but he has

DIAGRAM 3.1. Aspects of the Image of God in Men and Women

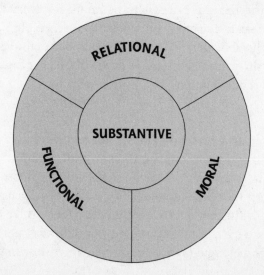

delegated to humanity a certain responsibility to manage or steward the world on his behalf. The image of God consists of those powers and apti- tudes (powers of reason, linguistic sophistication, memory, and so on) that enable people to perform these God-like functions.

This view of the image of God certainly has some merit, but is insufficient by itself. Its deficiency is exposed whenever humans, through injury or advancing age, lose their normal functional powers. Some secular ethicists today are prepared to deny the humanity of per- sons whose abilities to perform were lacking from the beginning, or have deteriorated and fallen beneath some arbitrarily established threshold. Generally, Christian ethicists have insisted that the image of God attaches to the essence or substance of every human being, regardless of ability or functional capacities.

The Substantive

As just stated, the universal human claim on the image of God does not appear in Scripture to be conditional on any tests of performance ability. According to Genesis 9:6, murder was a capital offense because it was the destruction of the image of God. This piece of theological ethics was not conditional upon the functional abilities of the victim of violence. Regardless of the degree to which humans lose their capac- ity to perform, they never cease to be human. It is always wrong to dehumanize such persons with labels like "vegetable," and to deny them the rights to which their enduring humanity entitles them. They continue to share in the substantive image of God because they are still members of the human race.

The Moral

A third and related perception of the image of God is that it is *moral*. To be God-like is to be someone who understands the difference between right and wrong, has genuine freedom to choose between the two, and must then take responsibility for the choices made. Humans are not simply the products of deterministic forces. Like God himself, humans possess a measure of transcendence, if only a small measure of it. Though belonging to the earth, humanity somehow transcends nature's closed system of cause and effect. Humans are genuinely free and undetermined in the choices they are called to make. Humans are a cosmic miracle.

Additionally, viewing the image of God as moral means that God-like humans should make the same kinds of moral choices God makes, as revealed supremely in Christ. By doing so, people will increasingly mirror the holy character of God in their lives. Much of the New Testament's call for a restoration of the image of God (see Rom. 8:29, for example) has this moral sense of the image of God in view.

As we continue, it is worth keeping in mind that the image of God, in all its aspects, is possessed equally by women and men. Neither gender is superior (or inferior) to the other in any functional, substantive, or moral sense. In other words, women and men are peers when it comes to what they can *do*, who they *are*, and how well they can *handle* freedom and responsibility.

The Relational

The fourth aspect of the image of God is the *relational*. The origins of this view lie in the close proximity of two very significant statements in Genesis: first, that humanity is in the image of God, and second, that humanity has been created male and female. These two affirmations are found together in two of the only three explicit Old Testament references to the image of God (Gen. 1:26–27; 5:1–2). The dynamics of our experiences of being-in-relationship, including those with God and with one another as male and female, are meant to reflect and imitate something of the interior life of the triune God. The image of God means not only that human beings have the *potential* to enjoy quality interpersonal relationships with God and others, but that they *actualize* such potential. The triune God is love, and, as Emil Brunner has explained it, "man cannot be man 'by himself'; he can only be man in community. For love can only operate in community, and only in this operation of love is man human."[5]

The pronoun designating God is deliberately plural—"let *us* make man in our image"—and God's plurality is imaged or reflected in a "pluralized" humanity composed of male and female. The form of

God's proposal to create humans is also worth noting. "Let us"—it is framed as a proposal that *invites* participation rather than demands it. It is an invitation to voluntary involvement rather than a pronouncement of what has already been decided. With this familiar and seemingly innocuous phrase, the author of Genesis pointedly underscores both "the non-solitariness of God on the one hand and His free agreement with Himself on the other."[6] The theme of complete freedom within God's unified being is an important one to which we will return shortly.

We were designed to be-in-relationship with God and one another in this distinctively God-like way. And while all our experiences of human community should aspire toward this Trinity ideal, the transformation begins in the primary relationship between a man and a woman. In that relationship, difference is obvious and should be accepted and celebrated. Union and harmony must never be sought through the suppression of liberty or the denial of individuality. It is to be accomplished through the higher, difficult, and more elusive experiences of equality, freedom, and mutuality.

The relational meaning of the image of God reminds us how closely the divine design for humanity is connected to the interior life of the triune God. How we relate to one another as women and men may be one of the most significant criteria by which our God-likeness can be judged to be restored. A while ago, a Christian man rather proudly explained to me the dynamics of his marriage and how he believed his firm exercise of male leadership solved all sorts of potential problems. "Now suppose the wife and I get home from work really tired," he began. "We're both hungry, but (we) don't feel up to cooking. So we decide to get take-out. She feels like Chinese, but I want Mexican. So . . . ," he said, pausing for effect, "problem solved! We get Mex." One can only imagine the joy at their kitchen table. Sadly, it is such a far cry from the pattern God models within himself.

The three persons of the triune God relate to one another in love, for God is love (1 John 4:8). On this basis some Christian theologians suggest that the persons of the Godhead share an "I-Thou" relationship. A what? I know "I-Thou" sounds very archaic, and few people in

America, outside of Amish country, typically talk like this anymore. Nevertheless, this strange term has a very relevant meaning. It signifies that the persons of the Godhead do not relate to one another as functionaries, or as officers of a corporation with defined job descriptions. Rather, they relate to one another in a directly personal way. They do not guard their privacy by only disclosing the minimum necessary to keep their organization or business operating smoothly. Instead, they are fully present to each other and relate, as we say, face to face.

Another way of expressing this dynamic is to say that they relate to one another as *subjects* rather than objects. A subject is free and responsible in a way that an object is not. A subject is able to initiate and to respond, and is prepared to do both. A subject enjoys the dignity of being unconstrained in choosing how to respond to invitations and opportunities. And yet, despite all the latent potential for division in genuine "I-Thou" relationships, we discover, to our wonder, that there is unity and harmony in the triune God.

Controlling Behavior Undermines Friendship

In the inner life of God we see what we were meant to be. We know from experience that controlling behavior negatively affects the quality of any human relationship. We also know that we treasure reciprocal friendships over the power-based grids within which we are often obliged to function as bosses and employees in the workplace. Even parent-child relationships, which are often the most precious that humans can experience, are designed to evolve beyond the early dynamics of parental command and child obedience. They are supposed to attain a more mature stage at which respect and affectionate caring survive, but the need for control has faded away. Where overt control or subtle manipulation persists into the child's adult life, the relationship is always judged to be dysfunctional.

Kevin remembers a summer Saturday night years ago. He was cruising around town with three other guys. The scene was straight out of *American Graffiti* or *Happy Days*. They were all trying hard to look cool. After a stop or two at the local drive-in, Kevin got bored with their tight little cruising circuit. "I think I'm ready to go home now," he announced from the backseat. His good friend Al, who was driving, appeared to ignore him. A few minutes later Kevin repeated his request to be dropped off. That's when Al finally responded. "You're doing nothing of the sort," he declared. "We're in this together for the whole night, so just sit back and shut up."

Until then Kevin had considered Al his best friend, but his reaction did not fit with Kevin's idea of a healthy friendship. He felt like he was locked in the back of a Mafia limousine "Excuse me?" Kevin retorted, his voice rising with emotion. "If you want me for a friend, pal," he announced, "you'll need to get rid of your gangster impersonation. Take me home, or pull over and drop me off, right now."

Grudgingly Al backed down, and Kevin eventually got home, still mad. But that night he learned a lesson he took with him for the rest of his life. Controlling behavior is always an assault on a person's God-like freedom and dignity, and it is especially inappropriate in friendships between equals.

God is a Trinitarian fellowship of holy love. Humanity was created to be like him, and the likeness was intended to extend to, and perhaps consist primarily of, social dynamics similar to those within the Trinity. The revealed ideal for human relationships is a mutuality of free persons united in self-giving love. An absence of power struggles and competitiveness, and of hierarchical structures to restrain them, is a hallmark of the genuine image of God. This is the ideal toward which humanity should aspire. The journey toward this ideal must start with, and be reflected in, the basic human relationship of male and female.

On Assignment Together

As we have noted, the first chapter of Genesis gives the big picture of God's creation of the universe, with special attention to planet Earth. The progressive steps of creation reach their apex on the sixth day with the creation of humanity (lit. *adam*, the human or earthling). This singular humanity was created, like almost all the other species already in existence, as a gendered duality of male and female (1:27). In Genesis 1 the Hebrew term *adam*, which in English has been almost universally translated "man," is actually a collective noun that embraces the male and female equally. Neither has a privileged claim on the designation "human." They are equally human.

Humans were then commanded to be fruitful and increase in number, to fill the earth and subdue it, and to rule over ("have dominion over," KJV) the other creatures (Gen. 1:28). This mandate was assigned to both the male and the female alike. It was humanity as male and female that God commanded to be fruitful, to subdue the earth, and to rule over all other life forms. No division of labor, no distinction between the marketplace and the domestic sphere, is indicated. No sphere of productive and fulfilling activity is off-limits to either the male or the female by reason of their gender. The mandate to multiply and be fruitful is one that involves both the male and female together. A natural reading of the text is that similar joint effort is envisioned in the other spheres of human endeavor.

Finally, the author of Genesis appears intent on highlighting the plurality of humanity. Clearly other species had already been created along male-female lines, but humans are the first creatures for which the issue of sexual differentiation is made explicit: male and female he created "them" and blessed "them" and spoke to "them" (1:27, 28). When we factor in the earlier statement of the Creator's own plurality ("Let *us* make human beings in our image" [v. 26 TNIV]), it is reasonable to conclude that the dynamic of maleness and femaleness within a single human solidarity is a significant part of what it means to be like God. We must conclude that how males and females relate to one another is of profound importance and should be patterned after the interior life of the One who is also social.

Enter Adam and Eve

The second chapter of Genesis focuses on the creation of humanity. From the macrolevel perspective provided by Genesis 1 we zoom in for a closer look at events during the latter part of the sixth day of creation. This is the section popularly known as the story of Adam and Eve. Our interest would be piqued, but not as intensely, if Adam and Eve were merely historical individuals. The thing that makes this narrative of such tremendous importance is that they function as *representatives* of their respective genders.[7] Adam has been taken to represent every man, and Eve to represent every woman. The Christian tradition of viewing Adam and Eve as archetypes has given these stories power to shape our assumptions about sex and gender.

Here we learn that man was created from the dust of the ground, which helps to make sense of the link between the Hebrew word for *earth* (or soil) and the word *Adam* (literally, earthling). For the first time we learn of a time interval between the creation of the male and the female. During this interval a number of things happened. Adam was assigned the task of working the garden of Eden and taking care of it. He was instructed concerning the tree of the knowledge of good and evil. He was asked to name all the other creatures, and presumably, to keep his eye open as he did so for a partner for himself. As it turns out, his search ends in futility. Nowhere in the rest of creation can he find a true partner.

God does not consider the male's solitary existence a satisfactory long-term arrangement. "It is not good for the man to be alone," says God. The text does not tell us exactly why Adam's solitude is unsatisfactory. Readers are left to ponder whether the problem was the daunting demands of the gardening job, Adam's inability to reproduce on his own, his struggle to obey the fruit ban on the one tree all by himself, or simply his need for a friendly companion. Perhaps it was a combination of these things.

Regardless, God anesthetizes Adam, and then removes a rib from his side, and from this rib fashions a woman (*ish-shah*, literally "out of the male") and presents her to Adam. He is delighted and recognizes her to be one with him and his equal: "This is now bone of my bones and flesh of my flesh; she shall be called 'woman,' for she was taken out of man" (Gen. 2:23). It is sometimes argued that according to ancient Near Eastern culture the act of naming another was an act of power. Even if such assumptions prevailed at the time Genesis 1–3 was written, "woman" is not Adam's *name* for Eve but simply his recognition of their equality of essence. The first time he actually *names* the woman is when he designates her as Eve (the mother of all the living), and this occurs *after* the fall and after God's prediction that Adam will oppressively rule over her (3:16).

The author of Genesis seizes the teachable moment here to provide a comment on marriage: "For this reason a man will leave his father and mother and be united to his wife, and they will become one flesh" (2:24). The point is that the relational dynamic between marriage partners is meant to reflect the perfect equality of nature that men and women have shared since the creation. Moreover, the fact that the man, contrary to the prevailing norms of ancient Near Eastern culture, is called here to leave his family and go to his wife, instead of the other way around, as patriarchal systems would have it, underscores the view that the author of Genesis is making a countercultural statement about gender equality in God's eyes.

Traditional Spin on the Story — Being First Matters

Unfortunately, there has been a tendency to interpret this biblical narrative through patriarchal spectacles. This view assumes that in moral matters God deals directly with the male (because Adam received instruction about the tree before Eve was created), and that the male has an obligation to instruct his woman on moral issues and to supervise her moral behavior (because the following chapter, Genesis 3, implies that Adam had informed Eve of God's warnings). The male is duty-bound, then, to be the spiritual priest of his family in a way that the wife can never be. Moreover, the fact that Adam performs the naming of the creatures by himself (and prior to Eve's coming) suggests responsibility for earthly stewardship and governance lies primarily with the man, and only to a lesser degree with the woman.

Because Adam was created before Eve, often it is inferred that every subsequent male possesses intrinsic superiority and a divine right to lead females. There are actually references to such thinking in the New Testament itself, and we will address these passages later. But remaining for now with Genesis 2, the male's status in relationship to the female has commonly been interpreted as though the ancient notion that the firstborn should always be privileged (the so-called theory of primogeniture) applies in this case. The passage also indicates that

God's solution to the problem of Adam's solitariness was to make "a helper suitable for him" (Gen. 2:18). Traditional patriarchal interpretation of this passage sees the woman's role as that of a dutiful assistant and servant of the man. She exists to meet his needs and make his life more pleasant. She exists and is there, in short, *for* him.

Though reading the second creation story along patriarchal lines is a time-honored practice, it is nonetheless mistaken. It takes off from cosmetic form and neglects the deeper meaning. To understand the author's intent in Genesis 2, we have to see that the theme of the chapter is not distinctions between the superior male and the derivative female. The dominant theme is exactly the opposite—their profound and remarkable equality of being, and God's desire that this equality be experienced in a special relational unity. When properly interpreted, Genesis 1 and Genesis 2 are both seen to breathe an identical and genuinely egalitarian spirit.

One of the stronger proofs of supernatural inspiration here is that the intent of the passage—to affirm male-female equality—ran so much against the grain of the accepted social order of the ancient Near East. It is remarkably countercultural—astonishingly so, in fact. It staggers the imagination to believe that an ancient writer "just thought it up." The chronological primacy of Adam in the creation story is of no real consequence. It is an incidental feature of the narrative, an element of the literary setup, merely a prop for the play.

A Partner Corresponding to Him

The interval of time between Adam's creation and Eve's is not meant to privilege Adam in any way. Rather, the story required a time lapse between the two to demonstrate the deficiency of life without otherness and gender diversity. By himself the male is not adequate, and his existence alone is less than ideal. What he really needs, and what God graciously provides is an *ezer kenegdo* (Gen. 2:18, 20).

We must start from this Hebrew term itself, since how it has been translated into English has been so ideologically charged. The venerable King James Version speaks of Eve as "an help *meet* for him," the old English way of saying that she was a helper fitting or *suitable* for him. For centuries now we have gotten it (erroneously) into our heads that the KJV describes Eve with the hyphenated noun "help-meet." The New International Version, the Bible of choice for many evangelicals, improved matters by translating the phrase as "a helper suitable for him." However, the Contemporary English Version did even better by changing this to "a partner suitable for him." Its substitution of "partner" for "helper" further reduces the likelihood that readers will assume any undertone of female subordination here.

We can get a clear understanding of the meaning of the original Hebrew term *ezer kenegdo* if we consider the two words separately: first the noun *ezer* and then its adjective *kenegdo*. As indicated above, the term *ezer* has been variously translated in English as "help," "partner," and "helper." Contrary to the patronizing spin often put on this Hebrew term in English translation, it conveys no hint whatsoever of female inferiority. If anything, just the opposite is the case. In terms of its theoretical range of possible meanings, the word *ezer* can designate an inferior (like a servant), an equal (like a partner), or a superior (like God). The point is that help can come from above, beside, or below— *ezer* itself does not discriminate.

DIAGRAM 3.2. Eve in Relationship to Adam:
Possible Translations of the Hebrew *Ezer Kenegdo*

EVE	=	*ezer*	*kenegdo*
GOOD	☐	help	meet for him
BETTER	☐	helper	suitable for him
BEST	☑	partner	corresponding to him

It is of at least passing interest that the term *ezer* is used most frequently in Scripture to describe God's role as the mighty helper of his people. This is not to suggest that as his *ezer* the woman is actually superior to the man. To indulge in such ideas does not bring us closer to the biblical ideal of gender mutuality, and may actually encourage a kind of reverse sexism. I simply note the fact to underscore how unlikely it is that *ezer* implies here that the female is an inferior or subordinate helper.

In this particular text, an equal helper is in view. This is the assumption that best fits the overarching theme of the chapter. But the clinching argument is the adjective *kenegdo*, which is best translated "corresponding to," or as one you relate to face to face (that is, as your equal). This is not the language an author would choose to describe a Girl Friday or helpful assistant. The meaning of the phrase may best be conveyed as "a partner corresponding to him." The translation "corresponding to" is preferable to "suitable for him." The former phrase correctly suggests an ontological and factual equality. The latter notion of "suitable for *him*" conjures up unfortunate visions of a woman's worth being judged by whether or not she gives the man pleasure and meets his needs. Once properly understood, then, the meaning of *ezer kenegdo* is thoroughly egalitarian.

Such a partner corresponding to the man could not be found anywhere else in all of creation. The solution was to form this partner from the very flesh and bone of the man himself. The point of the female's derivation from the male was not, as some patriarchal types would later claim, to establish the female's inferiority and dependence upon the male, but actually to underscore their equivalence in essence and substance. The point here is analogous to one made centuries later by the Nicene Council when it decreed that Christ was of the same substance as the Father. This is how Adam understood the situation when he exclaimed: "This is now bone of my bones and flesh of my flesh" (Gen. 2:23). Just as Adam was created out of the earth, and ever after existed as an earthy mortal, so the woman, created out of the man, claimed an equal share of his humanity. Adam recognized that he and the female were of one flesh.

Partners in Everything

The only remaining question is this: For the fulfillment of what divine mandates did Adam need assistance and aid from the woman? Obviously the Genesis 1 mandate to procreate was one he would have difficulty fulfilling unilaterally, but that is not part of the Genesis 2 narrative. God's prior command in Genesis 2 is to work the garden and take care of it. Most Bible commentators understand this to be a metaphorical reference to God's broader call to steward and manage the earth. Otherwise, Adam and Eve's subsequent expulsion from the garden would have left them unemployed! The most natural reading of the text, then, is to conclude that the woman, as a helper corresponding to the man, and as his equal, is to partner with him in the fulfillment of the creation mandate in its broadest dimensions.

Thus it never disappoints God when a woman serves as a chief executive officer, an owner, a head of state, a judge, a district attorney, a doctor, a research scientist, or a university president. Such women are not taking jobs away from men, as though men have a higher priority claim upon them. God is pleased when women perform with skill the highest duties in business, industry, government, health, or education. For in the beginning God assigned all dimensions of creation care to men and women without distinction.

The Night of the Sandbags

Plenty of snow remained on the ground when we were blindsided by a mini heat wave. Everything began to melt at once. The riverbeds and gullies filled up fast with churning brown water. Within a couple of days we had a full-scale flood on our hands. A large part of the city of Regina, the capital of Saskatchewan, was at risk. The local government sent out an emergency call for help. We heard it first on the radio. The chance to be useful in a time of crisis stirred something deep inside. We dropped what we were doing and headed straight for the designated response center.

We found ourselves borne along in a stream of citizens numbering in the thousands. They arrived from every walk of life and immediately set to work. They helped home owners salvage valuables, filled sandbags by the hour, and stacked them up against rising water at key points citywide. It was back-breaking work, and it continued day and night. Volunteers moved around freely in the open backs of city gravel trucks—exhausted, yet strangely upbeat. The Salvation Army provided coffee and snacks. We were on a mission together.

Past midnight an enormous mountain of sand glowed under makeshift lights while volunteers scurried all over it. Urgently they filled, tied, and loaded sandbags for the fight against the rising water. A uniformed policeman shoveled sand into a burlap bag held open by a bewhiskered street person—the two oblivious to the striking contrast between their respective appearances and stations in life. A grandmother worked with a teenage boy. Men and women, native Americans and whites, blue-collar workers and executives labored together, their hands raw from the work—freely doing what needed to be done. No one played the boss. No one cracked the whip. They set aside rank and status that night. They forgot about all that in their shared desire to save the city.

In time the water abated, and the city returned to normal. Unfortunately, "normal" also meant a return to pettiness. We resumed our former quests for status and control. We became preoccupied again with establishing our turf, protecting our egos, and carefully delineating everyone else's appropriate roles. Yet for one night it had not been about who was fit to lead, and who wasn't. Though I did not recognize it at the time, we had experienced something better—a fleeting glimpse of God's design for life together as men and women. We had witnessed joyful nonhierarchical partnerships in a cause of great significance.

chapter summary

The eternally triune God chose to create humans, male and female, and to confer upon them the great honor of imaging God's own being. The fact that Adam showed up first, and Eve second, is incidental to the teaching point of the story. She was a fully equal "partner corresponding to him." These first humans were intended to be like the triune God in all their relationships, and preeminently in how they related to one another as male and female. And so for a time Adam and Eve worked, discussed things, made decisions, and enjoyed life together on an undistorted basis of perfect equality, complete freedom, and enriching mutuality. In a word, it was heavenly.

Questions for Individual or Group Reflection

1. What makes humans unique among God's creatures?

2. Do women and men possess the substantive, functional, and moral aspects of the image of God *equally*? Discuss the implications of your answer.

3. Ideally, how would it look if people imaged God *relationally*?

4. Is God male? Summarize your reasons for thinking as you do.

5. What are the three possible meanings of the word *ezer*? How should we understand Eve's original role and relationship to Adam?

6. Review the claims from Scripture that Eve was created Adam's equal in every way. Which arguments, if any, do you find most persuasive, and why?

chapter 4

What Went Wrong

sin and the roots of gender oppression

I loathe snakes. Always have. I vividly remember from childhood a family hike one hot summer day to an abandoned farm in rural Ontario. There amid the high grass and weeds we found what had once been the farm's private water supply, an old well. When we slid its wooden lid aside, we discovered, instead of fresh water, a dark, damp pit containing a writhing mass of snakes. It made my skin crawl. It still gives me chills to watch that scene in *Raiders of the Lost Ark*, where Indiana Jones and his partner are trapped in the snake-infested depths of an Egyptian pyramid, while sinister cobras glide effortlessly through human skull eye sockets. Most people have an aversion to snakes (probably rooted in a primitive survival instinct); some of us just feel it more strongly than others. But the point I'm leading up to is that there was a serpent in the garden of Eden. In spite of the chronological and geographical distance from us, this serpent has had an enormous impact on our lives.

Having described the idyllic state in which the first man and woman lived, Genesis takes an ominous turn in chapter 3 with the appearance of the crafty snake. Here we catch our first glimpse of what went so tragically wrong at the outset of human history, and the catastrophic consequences that followed. The biblical account of the fall is one of the most significant and enduring of all the stories to shape human consciousness. For this reason it is critical that we interpret it properly.

An important aspect of Adam and Eve's imaging of God was the fact that both were free moral agents. They were not locked into a prewritten script. Part of their dignity came from being responsible for the decisions they made. The presence of a single off-limits tree in the middle of the garden symbolized this (Gen. 2:16–17). The tree itself was not evil. Its forbidden fruit simply created the possibility of right or wrong choice-making. Without its presence Adam and Eve could be neither fully human nor truly God-like.

A Fresh Look at a Familiar Story

The snake first approached the woman (Gen. 3:1). Why the woman, and not the man? It is an important question, and one that will be addressed later on. But for now I will simply say that it was a convenient design feature for the plot, though only an incidental one—a mere piece of literary scaffolding to help the author present the inspired truths embedded in the passage. So the snake approached the woman and began to tempt her.

His insidious strategy advanced through three stages of escalating danger: he began by sowing seeds of doubt in her mind about what God actually said, then about the credibility of God's warnings, and finally about the benevolence of God's character (vv. 1–5). This is archetypal temptation. It has a timeless quality. And Scripture seems to suggest that men and women are equally vulnerable to such deceptions (2 Cor. 11:3).

The woman is enticed by the appearance of the forbidden fruit and the prospect of gaining greater knowledge by consuming it. She considers her options momentarily, hesitates, and then takes and eats. The fateful deed is done, but the story is far from over. She also gives some to her man, who is not far away—who, in fact, is with her—and he eats too (Gen. 3:6). Evidently it is important to the storyteller that they *both* choose, so what we have here is a literary structure that allows this to unfold before us. Neither can decide for the other. Each is an independent agent, with all the dignity and responsibility associated with this privilege. The issue was never who sinned first.

With this pair of disobedient acts, Adam and Eve's innocence comes to an end. They feel shame for their nakedness and attempt to cover their bodies. They are afraid, and try, pathetically, to hide from their creator. But God calls out and in doing so addresses himself first to the man, Adam: "Where are you?" As the story continues, the two are located easily enough, and as they tumble out of the bushes their secret tumbles out with them.

In his wide-eyed desperation, casting about for an escape, Adam turns and scapegoats his partner, and indirectly reproaches God at the same time: "The woman you put here with me—she gave me some fruit from the tree, and I ate it" (v. 12). The man is implying that God and the woman are at fault, not himself. His response—the first recorded expression of his now fear-filled, fallen nature—is a telling one. By blaming his partner, he drives a wedge between himself and the one who is bone of his bone and flesh of his flesh. The roots of historic gender alienation are sown precisely here. Eve behaves no better. She tries to duck blame by passing it along to the serpent. By pleading that she had been deceived she attempts (unsuccessfully, as it turns out) to evade responsibility for her own choice.

This passage has stimulated more than its share of anti-female (misogynist) judgments and attitudes. It has been widely assumed that the serpent (aka the Devil) approached the woman, rather than the man, because he calculated that the woman would be less discerning, and morally less able to resist his temptation, than the man. By craftily approaching the *woman*, so the idea goes, the serpent focused his attack at humanity's weakest point. The success of the serpent's effort confirms this prejudice. Examples from Philo and Ben Sirach show that the rabbinic tradition tended to infer from the account of the fall that women were by nature more vulnerable to deception than men. Eve was made out to be the Edith Bunker of ancient Mesopotamia.

In traditional Christian thinking, Eve has been treated as the female archetype, not just an unfortunate woman who ruined things for herself. The conclusion followed that women, as "daughters of Eve," are intellectually and morally inferior to their male counterparts. They should not teach or exercise leadership, since positions of authority would widen the scope of their potentially damaging influence. Moreover, Eve set the pattern of the female as seductress or *femme fatale*, the one who through her irresistible enticements brings the poor man down to destruction. Conversely, Adam, as the archetypal man, introduced sin to the world by listening to a woman instead of instructing her and setting her straight. And the fact that God subsequently addressed Adam first, and held him responsible for things, is taken to mean that men have a proprietary or priestly role in relationship to their women in spiritual and moral matters.[1]

These have been the most common interpretations of Genesis 3, and ones which have had devastating consequences for the cause of gender equality, freedom, and mutuality in the Christian tradition. There are vestiges of these very attitudes on record even in the New Testament itself, and more will be said about this problematic fact. Such views are deeply imbedded in our collective patterns of thinking. They inform the default settings of our psyches. They pop out in our unguarded moments. And they can be altered only by sustained commitment to cognitive restructuring and the illuminating work of the Holy Spirit.

Tuning In to the Story's Meaning

But the question that must be asked is this: Are these correct interpretations of the story of the fall? Do they reflect the true meaning of the inspired text? It is important to ask this because, as Kevin Giles astutely observes, "Texts are not self-interpreting. They are only symbols on a page until a human agent gives them meaning."[2] It is *readers* who interpret the tale. The story of the fall does not come to us with an official commentary providing an authoritative explanation of the inspired author's intended meanings. Neither the biblical story of the fall, nor the gender dynamics within it, is self-interpreting.

In the absence of an authoritative interpretation, we are left with a couple of options. One is to continue to indulge in "loaded" interpretations of the story—interpretations heavily colored by our personal perspectives and subjective biases—and claim divine authorization for them. The other is to try to reread the story in accord with what we discern to be the overall content, tone, and direction of what the Spirit of Christ is communicating to the church through the Scriptures as an entirety. This enterprise is certainly not without the risk of error, but it is the only responsible way forward. Our best chance of getting it right is to keep our imaginations reverently immersed in the thought-world of the Bible, and prayerfully tuned to the directional impulse of the Spirit who speaks through it.

So let's take a careful look at the story in Genesis 3 again. We come back to the question we deferred earlier and ask ourselves about the significance of the fact that the woman, as opposed to the man, succumbed to temptation first. What is really going on here? And what are we to conclude is the inspired "teaching" of this ancient passage? Several considerations ought to make us pause before jumping on the traditional bandwagon of woman-blaming.

To begin with, it is unclear from the passage whether the serpent finds the woman by herself or simply chooses to engage her in conversation while Adam is present with his partner and listening in. Initially Adam is not mentioned, but in verse 6 we are surprised to discover him present. There is no reference to his arrival midway through the story. Seamlessly, it appears, the woman who had just eaten of the forbidden fruit turned and gave some of it to her husband "who was with her." She doesn't wait for him, or go looking for him, as we might expect if the author was trying to say that the chronological spacing of the two fatal acts was important. No, Eve just turns and there Adam is.

Both the King James Version and the New International Version note that Eve, in the act of eating, "also" (not "then") gave some to her husband, who was with her. There is not even a chronological sequence to the two fateful acts of consumption. While technically the woman did sin first, the man's sin followed so soon thereafter—immediately, in fact—that the main point of the passage is clearly that they both sinned. The sequence of their respective actions was obviously not a big deal. This was not the original author's point. Most likely we are to understand that Adam was there all along, and had been privy to the discussion between the serpent and his partner. If so, he would have had ample opportunity, had he so chosen, to intervene in the unfolding events and to insist on obedience to the command of God before it was too late.

Traditionally, of course, Jews and Christians have read the passage quite differently. The serpent's craftiness (v. 1) has been thought to lay precisely in his plan to catch the gullible woman while her male head was not around to protect her from herself. This is the notion perpetuated through the centuries by everything from medieval artwork to contemporary Sunday school materials. But in fairness, this interpretation is shaped by patriarchal prejudice rather than judicious exegesis. The phrase describing Adam as the one "who was with her" implies that Adam was with her all along. Consequently, we should visualize the two of them actually eating together. The original author would probably be surprised by the historic inference that it matters theologically that Eve sinned first, that she was a sinner longer than Adam. The author would be shocked to learn that this has been taken as one of the important truths of the story.

Step back one pace and look at what brackets this passage at either end. At the front we have the creation account of Genesis 1 and 2, which offers an even-handed portrait of gender equality. Likewise, in the description of the judgments that follow (vv. 14–24) there is every indication that the punishment God inflicted was distributed equally and on the basis of matching culpability. Since even-handed treatments of gender bracket the story of the fall, it seems clear that the author never intended to apportion blame for the fall unequally between the sexes.

What this arrangement of material does do effectively, however, is *unravel* the sequence of the original creation that began with God, led to the fashioning of the man, and culminated with the woman. It is to this woman that the serpent then appeals, and through the fall sin quickly begins to corrupt her relationship with Adam, and then in turn their relationship with God. Creation ascends from God through man to woman; the effects of sin descend down the other side through these same relationships. Some commentators describe this as the *chiastic* (or, reverse mirror-image) structure of the narrative, and this by itself may be sufficient to account for the prior appearance of the woman in the story of the fall.

Blaming Women

It is equally implausible to argue that the woman's sin was greater or lesser than the man's sin. We are given no clue to any distinctive motivation for Adam's sin. Even if there was some merit to the woman's complaint that she was deceived into sinning, so that her sin was somehow less culpable, it constituted an appeal that Adam would have been equally entitled to make since he was with the woman throughout their encounter with the serpent. One has to question the traditional inference that we are supposed to view women as by nature more easily deceived than men.

Yet this is precisely where traditionalists have gone in their interpretation of this text. This particular spin was certainly circulating in New Testament times. But we must challenge this facile line of reasoning by suggesting that such an attitude seems to perpetuate the very kind of woman-blaming Adam himself engaged in when God called him to account after the fall. If God refused to recognize any merit in Adam's tactic then, we should refuse to concede any ground to its functional equivalent today. God refused to let Adam climb to higher moral ground in relationship to his partner, and we should likewise refuse to accept any comparable allegations today. Christian men who do this sound too much like Adam.

Why Does God Address the Man First?

The other question we have deferred until now is this: Why is God portrayed addressing his very first inquiry after the fall to the man rather than the woman? Or at least, why did God not address both of them together? The text says clearly that "the LORD God called to the man, 'Where are you?'" (v. 9). It has been popular through the years to infer that God, in seeking Adam out, was treating him as the moral kingpin of the story. The most popular application drawn for today has been that all men, like Adam their archetype, are to exercise authority in spiritual matters on behalf of the women for whose welfare they are responsible.

Consider with me an alternative interpretation that goes something like this. The command not to eat the forbidden fruit had been communicated to Adam prior to Eve's creation (2:16–17). If Eve was aware of the prohibition, it would have been because Adam had told her. A prudent judge will always be careful not to jump to conclusions, especially when serious charges are pending. Just so, God did not want simply to *assume* that Adam had taken his responsibility seriously to inform Eve of the divine fruit ban. God's safest and best approach, according to this thinking, was to call to account the one to whom the original instructions had been given. Perhaps by this point you're shaking your head.

Even though some may think there's merit to this speculation, it probably underestimates what the ancient author believed God was able to know, simply by reason of being God. We ought to be reticent about reading contemporary best business management practices into an ancient story like this. So once again, I believe, the more satisfactory explanation lies in recognizing that there are actually two chiastic sequences (that is, two reverse mirror-image arrangements) in Genesis 2 and 3. We have already noted the first of these. In Genesis 2, we went up a kind of ladder in the original human *creation* sequence, which began with God, who created Adam, then Eve. In Genesis 3 we went back down that same ladder, so to speak, in a *sinning* sequence: first Eve sinned, then Adam, and finally God shows up again. It is a nice, symmetrical poetic structure—a clean chiasm.

But the poetic pattern has not yet played itself out. It continues with a second chiasm, though with a minor wrinkle, for a new character has been added—the serpent. Up a second ladder the story now

DIAGRAM 4.1. Poetic Structure of Genesis 2–3

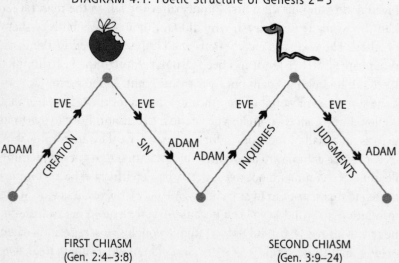

FIRST CHIASM
(Gen. 2:4–3:8)

SECOND CHIASM
(Gen. 3:9–24)

takes us, this time in a *divine inquiry* sequence. God goes looking for Adam and questions him first, then questions Eve, and finally turns to the serpent that started the whole fiasco (vv. 9–13). Finally, down this same second ladder we go again—this time in a divinely assigned *judgments* sequence. It is a simple case of last one in, first one out. The old serpent is cursed, then the woman is judged, and finally the man is punished (vv. 14–19).[3] And so with Adam the story of Genesis 2 and 3 comes full circle and ends where it began. The story has a fine crystalline architecture. There are good reasons why this is great literature as well as inspired Scripture.

Do you perhaps still think that Adam was being treated as the moral head of the first couple? Well, here's the clincher. When God finally connects with the furtive Adam, he does not hold him accountable for what *they* did, but only for what *he* did. God then turns to the woman and asks her to give an account of herself: "What is this *you* have done?" (v. 13, my emphasis). It seems very clear that Adam and Eve are treated as separate moral agents, each with a direct and independent relationship to God. If the author had intended to paint Adam as head of the house, the dialogue with God would have played out quite differently. No doubt Eve would have been marginalized from the awkward summit conference, and Adam would have represented them both. But instead Eve is treated as a real (albeit guilty) *person* in her own right.

The Judgments That Followed

God listened to the man and the woman and concluded that, their excuses not withstanding, both were guilty. God then responded in righteous judgment against the serpent first, then the woman, and finally the man. In each instance God's judgment involved a specific type of pain and predicts a specific form of alienation.

The serpent's pain is that it will have to crawl along the ground and eat dust. And God puts enmity between the serpent and humans; they will crush the serpent from above, the serpent will attack them from below (vv. 14–15). For her part, the woman will experience greater pain in childbirth, and her husband will rule over her. The original relationship between the man and woman will become poisoned by a toxic new dynamic of oppression and control (v. 16). As part of his judgment on the man, God curses the ground so that it will require painful, wearying labor for Adam to eke out a living from it. The man is alienated from the very earth from which he came. The death about which Adam had been warned is now inevitable, and the couple is temporarily cut off from any opportunity for immortality (vv. 17–19).

DIAGRAM 4.2. The Judgments That Followed in Genesis 3

GUILTY PARTY	PAIN	ALIENATION
the serpent	crawling and "eating dust"	from humans
the woman	difficult childbirth and husband-rule	from the man
the man	exhausting labor	from nature
the woman and the man together	doomed to die	from the tree of life

Though each divine judgment involves pain and predicts a dimension of alienation, God's judgments on the woman and the man are different. By focusing first on childbirth, God's judgment on the woman describes the consequences of sin on her domestic existence. By focusing on his struggle to earn a living from nature, God's judgment on the man pertains to his agricultural labors in the field. The consequences of sin would become legion and extend to every nook and cranny of the human condition, thwarting our yearnings for love, peace, and joy at every turn. The consequences recorded here are not the only results of sin; they are representative consequences which the author has chosen to highlight.

In these respective judgments, however, some Christians have detected a divine endorsement of a strict division of gender roles along these very lines. Women should birth babies and care for the home, while men should be the breadwinners and head out into the hurly-burly of the marketplace. Women belong in the private sphere, and men in the public. It is helpful, however, to remember that this narrative was written after the fall (we will leave it to qualified scholars to determine how long afterward). In any event, the story was not recorded on the spot, like a live CNN report. Thus it makes sense that the story reflects the gender roles that began to solidify later on in an agricultural society.

If the culture that produced the Scriptures had been primarily a seafaring one, like that of the Phoenicians, the judgment on Adam might have been that he would struggle with depleting marine stocks and empty nets as he tried to make a living in the fishing industry. If the story had been written with our culture in mind, Eve might have been advised that balancing her consulting business with homemaking duties would be an enormous struggle, and Adam would find himself exhausted, and at risk of heart attack, by the demands of the competitive high-tech industry. The point of these respective biblical judgments is that they confronted the man's and woman's lives with judgment at their respective centers, and in terms of the things that were most important to them at that time. The message was that the consequences of their sin would not be superficial or peripheral.

Gender Oppression Predicted

God's judgment on the woman deserves our special attention, especially because the outcome described has been a persistent feature of human society. We should make no mistake about it: right here is where gender hierarchy originated—not just dysfunctional hierarchy, but gender hierarchy itself. Prior to this specific moment of judgment there was no such thing. But here everything has changed, and it has changed for the worse. After mentioning the prospect of increased pain in childbirth, the passage concludes with the statement: "Your desire will be for your husband, and he will rule over you" (Gen. 3:16). The first part, "your desire will be for your husband," is particularly enigmatic, and interpretations range widely. Some traditionalists take it to mean that "your desire will be to usurp your husband's rightful position of authority." In other words, the fallen woman's desire or ambition will not be for her husband *per se*, but for her husband's *position*. Instead of being content with her proper place of subordination, she will be continually pressing to upset the natural order of things. Accordingly the follow-on clause, "and he will rule over you," simply means that the woman's ambitious schemes are futile. Despite her best efforts, she will never quite manage to dislodge the more powerful man. A future of frustrated ambition, then, is what she is doomed to endure.

This reading of the text encourages men to keep women in their place. But there are serious problems with it. One is that the Bible does not say that Eve's desire will be for her husband's God-given position. It says that her desire will be for her *husband*. In the second place, it begs the question of whether God had already conferred on the man a rightful position of authority over the woman. We maintain that there is no evidence that he did. The third problem is that the Hebrew word translated "rule over" carries particularly harsh connotations that cannot be reconciled with the original will of God in a perfect state.

A more plausible interpretation, because it flows so naturally out of what has come before, is to recognize that the clause "your desire will be for your husband" means exactly what it says—she wants her husband. The words describe the woman's yearning for a restoration of the relational intimacy that they enjoyed together in Eden. Tragically, that original life of harmonious mutuality is only a wistful memory now, and the woman is prepared to give up almost anything to restore a measure of it again. So great is this desire, history reveals, that the woman is sometimes willing to give up too much, including her own dignity, dreams, independence, and even self-esteem.

Yet despite how much she is prepared to relinquish for it, the dream remains elusive. Instead, the man rules over her. She seeks for a friend, but gets a master. The "ruling" described here is definitely not what God wants, or what God is recommending. What is being depicted here is the abuse of power, the sort of treatment that can best be described as oppression. If there is a biblical warrant for male leadership, it must be found elsewhere than in the tragic condition depicted here.

It is significant that patriarchy (or gender hierarchy) remains virtually universal in human societies. The global family of human cultures includes some matrilineal societies, and some matri-focal social structures, but it is hard to find many truly matriarchal (or female-*ruling*) ways of living. This state of affairs seems to be a simple case of "might makes right." In the absence of a countervailing belief system, the physically stronger and more violent will prevail in a way that the philosopher Friedrich Nietzsche understood all too well. Women are physically more vulnerable than men for a number of reasons. They possess less muscle strength, for example, and live with the competitive physical disadvantages of menstrual cycles, pregnancies, and prolonged maternal obligations. As a result they are more likely to be the victims than the perpetrators of sexual abuse, physical violence, objectification, and negative stereotyping.

Historically women have suffered from a double standard in sexual ethics, and have had fewer legal rights, less access to education and voting privileges, and less pay for equal work performed. The modern disciplines of history, sociology, and psychology help flesh out the full meaning and ramifications of the biblical phrase "and he shall rule over you." The oppression, which has its roots in man's sinful predisposition to exploit physical vulnerability, is reinforced and legitimized by patriarchal ideology. Perhaps the most insidious form of ideological reinforcement comes from religions that proclaim a divine endorsement of gender inequality and the oppressive consequences of this sort of thinking.

Does God Want the Suffering to Continue?

The concept of a curse is a withering and disturbing one. Both the serpent and the ground are explicitly cursed, but the passage before us stops short of saying that God *cursed* the man and woman as well. Nonetheless, the passage portrays God as an active agent of retribution in their cases as well. It is he who puts enmity between the serpent and the humans. It is God who greatly increases the woman's pain in childbirth, and evidently it is he who alters nature so that the man's subsequent labors in the field are arduous and exhausting.

It does this text a disservice to ignore or downplay the fact that it contains an explicit divine prescription. In other words, we need to acknowledge that God actually *prescribed* this judgment on Eve. It would be wrong to deny that there is a sense in which God personally willed these specific forms of judgments on the serpent, the man, and the woman. It evades the blunt force of the passage to dismiss everything it contains as merely predictive of what fallen humans will experience as the consequences of their actions naturally play themselves out in a world operating on automatic pilot. In the biblical worldview, God is not that detached and hands-off.

Yet having said this, it is difficult, impossible even, to decide exactly which negative outcomes are prescribed by God and which are merely predicted by him. And in the end this may not be the issue on which we should invest a great deal of energy anyway. We know that the passage is an expression of divine judgment on sin, but the more important issue is whether God wants men and women to *continue* to suffer along these lines.

The answer to that must be a resounding No! Christians celebrate the fact that God is *just*, but he is not only just. He is also, in Paul's great phrase, the *justifier* (Rom. 3:26). He is the merciful deliverer of those whom he was obligated to judge but never stopped loving. And ultimately his love finds a way to triumph over his judgment. From the moment of the fall onward, the God of the Bible—simultaneously just and loving— set a plan in motion to redeem humanity from the devastating impact of the original judgment. This is why, for example, we find the book of Revelation employing the imagery of a garden, complete with a fully accessible tree of life, to describe humanity's restored and blissful state (22:1– 5). Heaven is a full-circle return to Eden's glory and relational harmony.

Isn't it outrageous for Christians today to view male rule as something permanently prescribed by God? The holiness of God required that sin be judged, but the cross reveals that God is both just (thus the need for judgment) *and* the justifier (thus the subsequent provision of deliverance) of sinful human beings. Christ even became a curse (the *really* strong word) for us (for example, Gal. 3:13), so that such judgments as these in Genesis 3 would no longer apply to us. Redemption through Jesus Christ is more than sufficient to liberate women from even this sorry state of affairs. In Christ, women are now *beyond* the curse.[4]

And we need not wait for eternity to begin to experience a measure of this salvation. Even now, prior to the complete triumph of grace, God is at work in the world to correct the effects of the fall, including the relational estrangement experienced between men and women. While God's justice required that punitive measures be taken in response to the fall, God's loving heart spurs him to action to ensure that the effects of these measures are ameliorated and the pain they cause are reduced. Because he has always loved fallen humanity, God is pleased, for example, when medical means are found to reduce a woman's pain and risks in child-bearing. The science of obstetrics is not contrary to the will of God, but a means by which humanity can cooperate with the divine Healer. Like-wise, God is delighted when agricultural advances enable humans to sus-tain themselves with greater ease and joy in living, and when the dynamics of oppression in male-female relationships are reduced and even eliminated.

Even though God, as a just judge, was obliged to authorize these var-ious forms of pain and estrangement in the first place, the work of his kingdom has ever since been advancing to overcome them. It is not an affront to God to combat suffering. Just the opposite is true. And so we conclude that the prediction of man's rule over woman is a tragic conse-quence of sin. The man's "ruling" describes a way of relating between the genders which, though pervasive in history, can have no place in the king-dom of God. In light of this, it should also have no place in the church, which was designed to be a prototype of the kingdom and a witness of things to come.

There is just one last thing we should note here. As part of his dis-tributed judgments in response to the fall, God said, addressing the ser-pent: "I will put enmity between you and the woman, and between your offspring and hers" (Gen. 3:15). Often overlooked is the fact that the enmity is first of all between the serpent and the archetypal woman. Some skeptics regard this as little more than a bit of whimsical folklore to account for the perennial human phenomena of snake-phobia. But what if we take this serpent to be more than an ordinary snake? Suppose instead we take the serpent to be the personified embodiment of evil, as indeed it appears we should. According to this verse, then, Satan is at war with the woman, and as Madame Blocher-Saillens, a leading twentieth-century Bap-tist pastor in France suggested, "that war continues to the present time."[5] It is a sobering consideration that sexism may be one of the principalities and powers against which the people of God must wrestle today.

chapter summary

For awhile at least, the first humans got along like they were supposed to—without male supremacy, female submission, or differentials in power. Tragically, however, Adam and Eve used their God-given freedom to rebel, and thereby unleashed the corrupting power of sin on themselves and their descendants. The man and woman were *equally* responsible for this outcome. Among its countless tragic effects, which include death itself, was the mutation of original, God-like human relations into pathological ones of reciprocal blaming, interpersonal alienation, and gender oppression. Though not completely erased, the social image of God in the first couple and their offspring became seriously defaced.

[handwritten note: Not Male oppression, but Human oppression — Humans disobedience — The roots of oppression Human]

p Reflection

you always assumed

of Genesis 2 and 3?
in about the story?

nesis 3:16. Does God
ildbirth? Does he still

n. Is woman-blaming
examples.

5. How are men also suffering from the effects of the fall on gender relations?

CHAPTER 5

An Age of Patriarchy

GENDER PRIVILEGE IN THE OLD TESTAMENT

Do you recall the troubling story recorded in Judges 11 about an Israelite military leader named Jephthah? He was so anxious for victory in an upcoming battle that he made an exceedingly rash vow. In exchange for a guaranteed win, he promised God that he would sacrifice, as a burnt offering no less, whoever or whatever came out of his house to greet him on his return home. He won his battle against the Ammonites and, as it turned out, the first person to welcome him back was his innocent young daughter. He had absolute power to do whatever he wanted with this child. The culture gave him that. And he chose to keep his vow. Scholars are divided on the exact meaning of the biblical text at this point, but he probably killed her.

A Concubine on the Doorstep

Later on we read of a traveling Levite and his concubine, who found themselves at sundown near the town of Gibeah (Judg. 19). Eventually the sojourners found a place to stay, but local men soon started pounding on their door, demanding sex. The callous Levite gave them his concubine to abuse all night. In the morning he found her on the doorstep and ordered her to get up. It is unclear whether she was already dead or still dying. In any event, the Levite took macabre action. He brutally dismembered her body and distributed the pieces to the four corners of the land. We can only begin to imagine how awful the lives of women were. Welcome to the dark side of ancient patriarchy.[1]

Back to the Garden

The gospel is the good news of God's plan to overcome the consequences of his necessary judgment on sin and to restore humanity to
the conditions depicted in the first two chapters of Genesis. Salvation
in the biblical sense involves the hope of heaven, to be sure, but it is
about much more. It is about overcoming *all* the destructive effects of
evil, and in the imagery of the Bible itself, about returning to Eden.
Paradoxically, we had to look back to Genesis to get a clear vision of
the goal toward which the Spirit is leading us forward in redemptive
history. For the divine plan is to bring us full circle.

Getting back to the garden is turning out to be a long journey, and
we are definitely not there yet. In fact, the term "fall" is an especially
apt descriptor of what happened to humanity as a result of Adam and
Eve's sin. Collectively we fell into a pit from which we are still struggling to dig ourselves out. Afterward primitive humanity was pretty
much preoccupied with the struggle for sheer survival—life was nasty,
brutal, and short. The strong survived and flourished, while the weaker
were cowed into submission or enslaved. As Machiavelli would later
phrase things, might made right.

The original dynamics of egalitarian gender relations were profoundly perverted by sin's intrusion into human history. Women did not
fare well in ancient times. Vulnerable during pregnancy, burdened with
maternal duties, frequently victimized by men's superior muscular
strength, they saw their dignity erode and any residual claim to equality
with men wither away. Anthropologists point out that tribal life and societies characterized by physical violence, and the need to exercise brute
force in order to survive, are particularly fertile contexts for the triumph
of patriarchy.[2] Overall, the judgment recorded in Genesis 3:16 turned
out to be pretty accurate indicators of the way things were.

Patterns of Male Privilege in Ancient Israel

Patriarchy (literally, father-rule) designates any social order that
assumes male superiority and preserves male privilege. Salvation history began against such a social backdrop. The Old Testament illumi-
nates the way ancient Near Eastern women and men related during

this long span of centuries. It is important not to condemn the Bible as a sexist document for being honest and candid about this. It is a virtue, not a fault, to tell it like it was. A lot of the Old Testament is descriptive, not prescriptive. The Holy Spirit, speaking through Scripture, does not endorse everything that it reports. Likewise we ought to be careful not to treat all the social attitudes and practices *described* in the Old Testament as normative for today.

Israel's history consists mainly of stories of big men—Noah, Abraham, Isaac, Jacob, Joseph and his brothers, Moses, Joshua, David, and so on. The history of Israel is woven around the biographies of these Mount Rushmore–sized male figures. With God's help these men did exploits, and their women cheered about those feats, using tambourines instead of pom-poms. The all-important genealogies, by which family histories were remembered and identities created, were always patriarchal in structure.

Women appear in the stories, but (with few exceptions) as supporting cast, and quite frequently as persons lacking even names. Dinah, the one sister of Jacob's twelve sons, had no tribe named after her. She was the voiceless victim of a rape and, after being retrieved from the home of her attacker by her powerful brothers, slipped back into invisibility. When women did move briefly into the spotlight, as did Sarah, Hagar, Tamar, and Rahab, it was usually as relatively powerless persons in incidents related to their sexuality. More than anything, this latter point reflects what that society valued in women.

Women figure fairly prominently in the early Bible stories of Abraham and his immediate descendents. This was certainly true of Sarah, the mother of nations; Rebekah had some say in whether she would marry her cousin Isaac; and Jacob consulted both Leah and Rachel before deciding to return to the Promised Land (Gen. 17–31). The marriages of Abraham and Sarah, Isaac and Rebekah, Jacob and Rachel appear to have been characterized by genuine love and close interaction.

Still, the husbands were able to impose their wills on their wives, even in unconscionable ways, and get away with it. On two occasions the patriarch Abram relinquished his wife Sarai to the harem of a local ruler, and later on, as contemporary family systems theory might predict, his son Isaac adopted the same survival strategy with his wife Rebekah. In Sodom, Abraham's nephew Lot tried to buy off a local gang of thugs harassing his guests by offering them his two virgin daughters to rape as they saw fit. When it comes to exposing values and attitudes, such actions speak volumes.

In order to assert themselves, and sometimes just to survive, women had little choice but to be indirect and occasionally manipulative. Rebekah schemed to obtain the birthright for her favorite son Jacob. In the next generation, Rachel stole, and then deviously concealed, the idols of her father Laban as she and Jacob made their escape from him. Jael feigned hospitality toward the enemy general Sisera in order to drive a tent peg through his skull. Her story anticipates aspects of the beautiful Judith's coy deception and eventual beheading of the Assyrian general Holofernes in the apocryphal book of Judith. Likewise, to ensure their survival, Ruth and Naomi had to position themselves shrewdly, and eventually under cover of darkness, to secure the support of their male relative Boaz.

Concubinage and polygamy were normalized arrangements for male sexual expression. The role of concubine offered a woman more security than prostitution, but it still denied her the rights and security associated with a marriage contract. Polygamy was consistent with the assumption that a man was worth more than a woman. Both social arrangements fell well short of providing women with the security and equality possible through the still-future institution of permanent, monogamous marriage.

A double standard prevailed in sexual politics, as the story of Judah and his widowed daughter-in-law Tamar illustrates. Judah was about to have Tamar executed when her promiscuity was discovered; he was given reason for pause when told that he was the father of her gestating child. By the social standards of the day, he was not at risk of any punishment himself. His willingness to acknowledge the hypocrisy of this cultural double standard is perhaps the narrative's redeeming feature (Gen. 38).

The great shame of women was to be "barren"—without children. Sarah, Rachel, and Hannah are just three biblical examples of women who agonized over the problem of infertility. The dominant ideology of patriarchy located responsibility for such an impasse entirely with the woman. The enormous burden of shame and diminished self-esteem that accompanied female "barrenness" was due to the fact that procreation was a woman's chief means of contributing to society. There were few alternative ways to obtain fulfillment, significance, or public approval. In this light we can understand the depth of Rachel's cry to Jacob, "Give me children, or I'll die!" (Gen. 30:1).

Men Were In Charge

Public leadership in Israel, whether it was embodied in a judge, a monarch, or a military general, was almost always reserved for men. There was only one female judge in the history of Israel—Deborah, who led the nation in counsel and battle planning. Even she is still identified in her triumph as the wife of inconsequential Lappidoth (although some scholars think the Hebrew text actually means "woman of fire"). The patriarchal ethos of that time is reflected in Deborah's sardonic prediction of the eventual humiliation of Barak, her timid male associate in arms: "Because of the way you are going about this, the honor will not be yours, for the LORD will hand [the enemy leader] over to a woman" (Judg. 4:9). The exception proves the rule: women were not normally leaders, and it was shameful for any man to have a woman best him.

The age of monarchy, which succeeded the period of the judges in Israel, is memorialized in the historical books of Samuel, Kings, and Chronicles. Beginning with Saul, rising to great heights with David and Solomon, and then gradually declining through a north-south political rupture and a series of devastating exiles, the monarchy led Israel for many centuries. Almost without exception the national leaders were kings rather than queens. Men ruled Israel. The Queen of Sheba, a foreign queen, comes calling on Solomon, only to be dazzled by his superior wisdom and the splendor of his court (1 Kings 10; 2 Chron. 9). We are told that it was Solomon's many pagan, idolatrous *wives* who led him astray (1 Kings 11:3); once again, the female is responsible for the man's fall. The two women who figure most prominently in the biblical record of the monarchy years, Jezebel and Athaliah, are depicted as monsters.

Ruth, a Moabite convert, and Esther, an exilic Jew, are the only two women to have Old Testament books named in their honor. Ruth's story is one of inspirational faith and courage, as she follows her mother-in-law, Naomi, back to Israel and an uncertain future there. Her efforts are eventually rewarded with a good marriage, financial security, and (as the New Testament adds) the privilege of being a link in the genealogy of the Messiah. Centuries later Esther, a member of the exilic community of Jews, found herself catapulted into the role of wife of powerful King Xerxes of Persia. Imperial power and patriarchy coalesce in the Persian court in a way that left trophy wives perpetually at risk. Esther's vulnerability is clear to her and implicit in her famous statement of courageous resignation: "If I perish, I perish" (Est. 4:16). Like Ruth, Esther is a resilient woman who managed to survive and succeed in a highly patriarchal order.

Did Scripture Adapt to Local Conditions?

Everyone understands that the "host culture" in which salvation history began was patriarchal. It is harder to come to terms with the fact that God's revelation was adapted to this mind-set and social dynamics of male supremacy. The Old Testament is an inspired record of God's revealing and saving activity in human history. Through it, ethical monotheism is unveiled (the reality of one God who cares passionately about right and wrong), along with God's loving heart, his invitation to covenant, guidance in the path of life and peace, the assurance of a coming deliverer, and countless promises to inspire hope for the future.

Yet this supernatural revelation was thoroughly adapted in order to be understood and accepted by a male-dominated society. Even though women and children were expected to hear the Torah read (Deut. 31:9–13; Neh. 8:1–3), the law of Moses was written primarily with a male audience in mind and reflected a culture in which husbands had almost complete authority over their wives, and fathers over their daughters. A woman was not her own person in any civic sense. While the Old Testament law softened some of the more glaring injustices of ancient Near Eastern social practices, it perpetuated an uneven playing field between men and women. The divorce laws, for example, which Jesus would later attribute to the hardness of hearts, clearly favored the husbands over the wives (Deut. 24:1–4).

The covenants God made were almost invariably arranged with male representatives of the chosen people—men like Noah, Abraham, Jacob, and Solomon. Sarah was the beneficiary of a beautiful personal promise from God (Gen. 17), but it was mediated to her through her husband. God's promise to Abraham that *he* would become a great nation, and all nations would be blessed through him (Gen. 18:18), is typical of the larger pattern. While God frequently overruled the cultural assumption of firstborn privilege (primogeniture), the coveted divine "blessing" was still passed down through the male line from father to son.

The same held true in the sphere of institutionalized religion. Circumcision, the sign of the covenant, was a practice relevant only to male children in the community of faith (Gen. 17). The ritual consecration of all firstborn males (Ex. 13:1–2) was another divinely ordained Hebrew practice that reflected that society's valuation of the man over the woman. Along with the disabled, women were categorically excluded by the law from Levite offices and the priesthood (Lev. 6, 8) and regarded as unfit for those positions that represented the greatest proximity to God in the theocracy of Israel. The official fee for redeeming (that is, releasing from obligation) a man who had dedicated himself to the Lord was higher than (almost double, in fact) the fee for redeeming a dedicated woman (Lev. 27).

Male Readers Mainly in Mind

The form in which divine revelation was recorded also reflects the male dominance of the times. Men were the principal readers in mind, with women only addressed by association. The Law, given on Mount Sinai, is a good example. The Ten Commandments were progressive, inasmuch as they commanded Israelites to honor their mothers as well as their fathers (Ex. 20:12). And yet the commandments, and all the other supporting legislation, were still written with a male audience in view, as indicated by the tenth command not to covet one's neighbor's *wife* (Ex. 20:17). There is no parallel admonition to Israelite women not to covet their neighbor's husband.

Likewise the Psalms and wisdom literature of the Old Testament were written by men, and treat issues from a male perspective. The Psalms portray the hurly-burly of a man's world, and the kinds of fears and anxieties evoked by it. This is even more apparent in Proverbs, whose sage advice is directed to sons, and so stresses the pitfalls of sexual promiscuity and female seduction that one can see how it contributed to the perception of the woman as temptress. Parallel or equivalent forms of temptation that females might encounter are not given the same amount of attention.

The book of Proverbs concludes with an extended tribute to the noble and industrious wife (Prov. 31). The wife profiled in this passage is surprisingly active in public affairs and thus more liberated than we might expect from other passages of the Old Testament. Nonetheless, there is no parallel profile of the kind of husband for whom a wise woman ought to hold out. Proverbs is a man's book. It necessitates that women who wish to profit from it, and other portions of Scripture like it, must engage in a degree of gender translation or adaptation not required of male readers.

The Spirit Already Moving

Quite a bit in the Old Testament is not normative for Christians today. There are many ways in which it fails to reflect what ought to be. It sanctions the acquisition of slaves (Lev. 25:44), and even of a man selling his daughter as one (Ex. 21:7). It suggests what are now excessively severe penalties for sinful behavior: working on the Sabbath is punishable by death (Ex. 35:2), and so is even cursing one's parents (Lev. 20:9). Whole groups are exterminated, including innocent children and animals, for the sins of an individual or a few members of the group. Murderers like Moses and David were allowed to escape judicial consequences for their actions and continue to lead the people of God. Perhaps then we should not be so shocked that the Old Testament writers did not always display sensitivity to the plight of women. Even though they firmly grasped profound truths of divine revelation and communicated those with uncompromising courage and clarity, areas of their hearts and minds remained unenlightened.

Yet the Spirit was already on the move with respect to gender inequality. The Old Testament was instrumental in drawing Israelite social life, including its treatment of women, to a level above that of surrounding societies. It contained practices and teachings that elevated the dignity of women, and pointed in the direction of much more. The men in the ancient stories may not have felt much sympathy for women, but God was aware of their plight, cared about them, and reached out to them in merciful interventions. His response to the plight of Hagar, Abraham's Egyptian concubine, shows his concern and compassion. Rejected by all the people with power in her world, she is sent off to wander in the wilderness without resources or hope. Not once but twice God intervenes on her behalf. "The LORD has heard of your misery," an angel explains on the first occasion, and with deep insight Hagar gratefully responds: "You are the God who sees me" (Gen. 16:11, 13).

In ancient Israel, sons inherited the property of their fathers. When a man by the name of Zelophehad died, he left five daughters but no son. The daughters, evidently a spirited group, appealed directly to Moses for an exception to the existing inheritance laws. As women, they requested the right to inherit their father's property. So, the Scriptures say, Moses brought their case before the Lord, and the Lord instructed Moses that "what Zelophehad's daughters are saying is right" (Num. 27:1–7). The unprecedented ruling upset the existing order, but it signaled God's approval of movement in the direction of more rights for disenfranchised women.

In the time of the Judges a man by the name of Elkanah had two wives, and one of them, Hannah, was childless. She endured a great deal of taunting because of this and grew depressed. On a visit to the religious center of Shiloh, Hannah pled with God to intervene. He did, and enabled her to become pregnant. She gave birth to Samuel, who went on to become a great leader of Israel. The compassion of God led him to respond to a woman's greatest felt need, even though that need had been created and defined to some extent by the social stereotyping of a male-dominated society.

Champion of the Powerless

It is significant that spirited women in the Old Testament celebrated God as a champion of the powerless and the underdog. From their experiences these women understood that God was inclined to turn established patterns of power and authority upside down and orchestrate great reversals. After Israel's deliverance through the Red Sea, Miriam exulted that God had hurled the horse and its rider, symbols of Egypt's military superiority, into the sea and enabled a vulnerable people to go free (Ex. 15:21). The prayer of Hannah is likewise exultant: God "raises the poor from the dust and lifts the needy from the ash heap; he seats them with princes and has them inherit a throne of honor" (1 Sam. 2:8).

Mary, the mother of Jesus, stands in this tradition. Her feisty song is patterned after Hannah's and includes the declaration that God "has performed mighty deeds with his arm; he has scattered those who are proud in their inmost thoughts. He has brought down rulers from their thrones but has lifted up the humble" (Luke 1:51–52). Some people might perceive a hint of vanity in Mary's comment that "from now on all generations will call me blessed, for the Mighty One has done great things for me" (vv. 48–49). Actually, it is an expression of Mary's wonder that God would confer upon a simple girl from Nazareth the gift of significance. It was not something women were accustomed to anticipate. It was more than she had ever dared to hope for, but she was delighted to receive it nonetheless.

The Prophets Anticipated the Spirit

The ministry of the classical prophets was the high-water mark of Old Testament revelation. They believed that history was going somewhere—that is, that it had a trajectory—and that God's hand was upon the process.[3] Drawing out the deeper truths already implicit in the Law, their ministries were characterized by an intensified passion for social justice and an anticipation of greater things through an expanded future work of the Spirit of God. The prophets were outraged by morally compromised institutional religion and felt disdain for piousness that ignored the need for real-world social change.

They were alert to the ways power was being abused and the weaker members of society being exploited and crushed by those over them. To the prophets, the resulting social conditions were unjust, reprehensible, and intolerable. Amos claimed that God found Israel's religious practices despicable. Instead what he wanted from them was justice and righteousness: "Let justice roll on like a river, righteousness like a never-failing stream" (Amos 5:21–24). The prophet Micah put it this way: "He has shown all you people what is good. And what does the LORD require of you? To act justly and to love mercy and to walk humbly with your God" (Mic. 6:8 TNIV).

Few persons were more vulnerable in patriarchal society than women who had become man-less. Confined to the domestic sphere all their lives, and ill-equipped to earn a living in the public square, widows were especially at risk. From early on, Israel had been instructed to show compassion for the weak and disenfranchised among its citizens. And from early on, this was understood to include women who had lost husbands (Ex. 22:22–24). The prophets intensified this ethical demand, and worked hard to resensitize the conscience of the nation to the oppression experienced by widows, along with orphans, aliens, and other victims of poverty and powerlessness. The prophets were the original champions of a theology of liberation. In their advocacy of widows and orphans, they addressed the suffering of victims of a patriarchal order. They did not yet directly challenge the gender assumptions that supported that order, but in their sensitivity to the dynamics of power and oppression they laid a foundation for the next phase of the Spirit's trajectory.

The prophets realized that ethical progress required a greater manifestation of the Spirit's presence and power. The hardness of human hearts was the prime obstacle to personal transformation and social justice, but Ezekiel saw a day ahead when God would put a new Spirit within his people (Ezek. 11:19). Zechariah spoke for the entire prophetic cohort when he reminded the beleaguered governor Zerubbabel that it was "'not by might nor by power, but by my Spirit,' says the LORD Almighty" (Zech. 4:6).

The prophet Joel, resonating with these visions, predicted a day when God's Spirit would be poured out with unprecedented extravagance on all of God's people. "I will pour out my Spirit on all people. Your *sons and daughters* will prophesy, your old men will dream dreams, your young men will see visions. Even on my servants, *both men and women*, I will pour out my Spirit in those days" (Joel 2:28–29, my emphasis). It would deluge them all indiscriminately. The distribution will ignore traditional hierarchies based on seniority and sexism. The signature style of the Spirit is to be subversive of gender hierarchy, and we detect another early signal of this fact when we consider that three of the mightiest women in Israel's history—Miriam, Deborah, and Huldah—were designated as prophets. They were, in other words, persons who spoke and acted from a powerful anointing of the Spirit. Where the Spirit is at work, women will be at work.

Finally, the prophets looked ahead to a day when God would send a Messiah to deliver his people from every form of bondage and oppression brought on by human sinfulness. As the prophet Isaiah foretold in the words of the coming Messiah himself, "The Spirit of the Sovereign LORD is on me, because the LORD has anointed me to preach good news to the poor. He has sent me to bind up the brokenhearted, to proclaim freedom for the captives and release from darkness for the prisoners" (Isa. 61:1). Two central themes of the prophets converge in the Messiah's ministry: he will be Spirit-filled, and he will be intent on liberation. Great expectations surrounded the coming of this anticipated Messiah, and certainly not least for women.

The Era of the Rabbis

The four centuries prior to the advent of Christ were distinct in the history of the Jews. These were the post-exilic years, when a chastened Jewish nation tried to survive Greek and Roman invasions and struggled to maintain its identity in the face of relentless encroachment. Once tethered to the Promised Land, Jews were dispersed throughout the region of the Mediterranean and subjected there to great pressure toward cultural absorption and religious syncretism. Meanwhile "thus says the Lord" no longer resounded. No more Spirit-inspired writers emerged to produce texts worthy of canonical status. God had become silent.

DIAGRAM 5.1. Religious Authorities in Judeo-Christian History

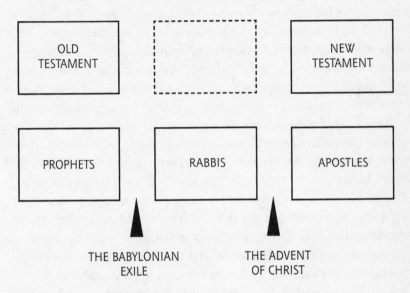

In the spiritual vacuum created by all of this, religious authority shifted into the hands of the teachers of the *existent* Scriptures, the rabbis and synagogue leaders, those who were the precursors to the Pharisees of Jesus' day. Thus began an extended period characterized by a relative silence of the Holy Spirit, a silence that would have a significant and regressive effect on the ethos of Judaism.

Extensive literary sources have survived from this period, which help to illuminate the sociocultural state of Judaism and, just as importantly, the thinking of the religious leaders of this time. It is a telling point that this body of literature was written, as far as we know, exclusively by men. Though a few books were written *about* women, the women of the times acquired no voice of their own. Nonetheless, such literary sources as these, along with related archaeological evidence, provide insight into the image and status of Jewish women on the eve of the Christian era. In response to the many external threats to Jewish religion and identity, rabbinic leaders gravitated toward more defensive, even reactionary, strategies expressed in conservative legislation. In general, this was not a time of positive developments for Jewish women.

Jewish women during this era took no part in public life and were restricted for the most part to being wives and mothers. Rabbinic descriptions of the ideal home atmosphere are actually quite attractive in their own way and depict benevolent patriarchy at its best. However, such domestic environments were sustained at considerable cost to women, who were to stay indoors as much as possible and avoid conversation with men. If they had to go outside, as poorer women were frequently obliged to do for various practical reasons, it was imperative that they venture out under head veils as essentially invisible persons. Annual religious festivals permitted the few exceptions to their sequestered lives.

A father's power over a daughter was virtually complete. He represented her in legal matters and arranged her marriage (although she could not be betrothed against her will). His authority transferred to the daughter's husband at the time of marriage. The husband thereby "acquired" her in the legal sense, and the social expectation was that henceforth she would obey him as her master. Polygamy was still permissible for men (though polyandry was not for women), and the right to divorce rested exclusively with the husband. It was a woman's special honor to give birth to sons. The absence of children was considered a great misfortune, even a divine punishment, for fertility was still the defining feature of a good woman.

Women continued to hold an inferior position in Jewish religion. They were exempt from obligation to observe religious festivals and even certain Sabbath restrictions. They did not matter enough for it to be otherwise. Moreover, it was not customary—in the cases of some rabbis, not even permitted—for women to lay their hands on the head of a sacrificial animal in the rituals of purification and forgiveness. Occasionally exceptions were made, but as one rabbi explained in the *Babylonian Talmud*, these were always just "to appease the women."[4]

A Woman's Place

At the center of Jewish religious life was Herod's temple in Jerusalem, an impressive edifice rebuilt on the site of the earlier and more fabled temple of Solomon. In his *Antiquities of the Jews*, the first-century Jewish historian Josephus described the temple site as a series of increasingly restricted-access courtyards as one moved from the perimeter toward the Holy of Holies at the center. The layout began with an outer courtyard open to Jews and Gentiles alike, then a court of women, beyond which women dared not venture, then one for Jewish men only, and finally one exclusively for the priests—the clergy of that day. Taken together, it was an architectural reflection of the stratified worldview of Pharisaic Judaism and an enduring reminder of the various divisions that were to become dissolved by the gospel. The court of women marked the limit beyond which women could not go to worship nearer the holy place. We find no such gender-segregated layout in any Old Testament descriptions of tabernacle or temple and conclude, therefore, that this may have been a rabbinic innovation in Jewish religious history.

A similar spirit operated in the evolution of design for synagogues, those satellite centers of Jewish life and faith in all the regions of the world to which Jews were increasingly dispersed. By the end of the first century, women were physically segregated from men in synagogue worship by screens, balconies, or other means. The good news was that women were still permitted to attend synagogue and listen to the reading of the Law. But the rabbis were inclined to distinguish between hearing the Law and seriously studying it.[5] With respect to the latter, one rabbi went so far as to suggest that the words of the Torah were better burned than handed to a woman.[6] When one considers how much Jews reverenced the Torah, this is quite a sentiment to express.

"Inferior in All Things"

Jewish women were also not encouraged to obtain an education, never mind devote themselves to the study of the Law. Rabbinic training took place in academies from which women were excluded. Men who were serious about their religion were discouraged from talking much to women or wasting time in conversation with them that could be better invested in study of the Law.[7] Little wonder that women's moral and intellectual abilities were not highly regarded. The cumulative evidence of male attitudes is quite disturbing. One rabbi generalized that "women are of unstable temperament,"[8] and Josephus claimed that women were unsuitable as witnesses because of "the inconstancy and presumption of their sex."[9] In *The Embassy of Gaius*, Philo, a prolific first-century Jewish scholar from Egyptian Alexandria, claimed that "the judgments of women as a rule are weaker and do not apprehend any mental conception apart from what their senses perceive."[10] In the same vein he suggested elsewhere that "in human beings the mind occupies the rank of the man, and the sensations that of the woman."[11] The perceived differential in value between a man and a woman is stated with brutal clarity in one rabbi's remark that when a man and woman are in danger, the man must be saved first.[12]

Likewise Josephus, in *Against Apion*, offers this opinion: "For, says the Scripture, 'A woman is inferior to her husband in all things.' Let her, therefore, be obedient to him; not so that he should abuse her, but that she may acknowledge her duty to her husband; for God hath given the authority to the husband."[13] We are not aware of the Scripture, to which Josephus refers, that teaches a woman's inferiority to her husband. But the statement is significant nonetheless. Clearly Josephus was familiar with a contemporary sexist interpretation of some particular Scripture passage and found that interpretation convincing enough not to question it. Most likely the text to which Josephus referred was the Genesis account of the creation and fall. It is interesting that a patriarchal spin on the Genesis narrative did not surface in the centuries prior to the emergence of the rabbinic tradition.

Ben Sirach was a Jewish scribe who operated an academy in Jerusalem around 180 BC. The distilled teachings of this man comprise the apocryphal book of Ecclesiasticus (also known as the Wisdom of Ben Sirach), in which he declares ominously: "Sin began with a woman, and thanks to her we all must die" (25:24 JB). The responsibility for sin and its consequences is laid disproportionately on Eve's shoulders. Likewise Philo, in his commentary on Genesis, believed the reason the serpent chose to tempt the woman first was because "the woman was more accustomed to be deceived than the man . . . because of softness she easily gives way and is taken in by plausible falsehoods which resemble the truth."[14] After the fall, the Genesis story describes God inquiring first of Adam, rather than Eve (Gen. 3:9). This, said Philo, was because "it was the more imperfect and ignoble element, the female, that made a beginning of transgression and lawlessness, while the male made the beginning of reverence and modesty and all good, since he was the better and more perfect."[15]

Taking into consideration all these realities, from the temple's layout to the sayings of the rabbis, it is little wonder that male Jews felt relief that they did not fall into any of the categories of inferior persons, including women. It comes as little surprise, then, that another great rabbi instructed men in daily worship to pray this way: "Blessed are you, God, for not making me a heathen [Gentile], a woman or a slave."[16] As R. T. France notes, Jewish men could use such words without embarrassment and, presumably, express them in the synagogue in the presence of women.[17]

Some have suggested that this prayer is simply an expression of gratitude for being able to study the Law of God seriously and is not really discriminatory at all. But the thinking expressed by this prayer appeals to human pride and the darker side of our nature, and some of that is explicit in the Talmud itself. These words epitomize a mind-set against which the apostle Paul would later take pointed aim in his privilege-dismantling gospel manifesto to the Galatians. These developments were clearly regressive and counter to the positive trajectory of the Spirit. Whenever the Spirit is muted, as it was in this era, there is a calcifying of organized religion and a numbing of spiritual sensibilities. This particular era of regression was real and serious, and not least for women. But happily the declension would not prove permanent.

chapter summary

The Old Testament provides a window into the patriarchy that prevailed in the ancient Near Eastern world and among the people of God. Divine revelation was adapted to this cultural mind-set, so that Hebrew life and religion, as well as the texture of the Scriptures themselves, have a patriarchal feel to them. But the renewing Spirit of God was quietly at work from the beginning, softening the harsher features of gender oppression at first, and then later, in the age of the prophets, sensitizing Israel to problems of injustice and revealing God's will that these be overcome. Following Israel's exile to Babylon, the ministry of the Spirit became muted for a time under the influence of legalistic rabbis. At this point in our story, we take comfort that it is often darkest just before dawn.

Questions for Individual or Group Reflection

1. Do you think it would be a good or bad idea to return to some of the gender practices of Old Testament times? Why or why not?

2. Much of the Old Testament is descriptive, not prescriptive. What do these terms mean, and why is the distinction between them important?

3. Do you think it ever takes an extra effort for women to apply Old Testament truths to their lives? Why?

4. Where can we detect signs of the positive trajectory of the Spirit?

5. Why is it significant that "daughters" are included in the prophecy of Joel 2:28–29?

CHAPTER 6

Jesus Christ and Women

the Launch of the gender revolution

Churchill, Manitoba is an isolated Arctic community on the rocky shores of Hudson Bay, way up at the tree line where the summertime sun barely sets. It was a surreal place back in the 1960s—and this teenager's dream destination. For a few fleeting months each summer, the ice cleared enough for ships to come in from the north to load grain from the Canadian prairie. White beluga whales cavorted in the bay (chased around by Inuit with shotguns in motor boats), while enormous polar bears casually ransacked garbage barrels around town. There were no roads into Churchill; almost everything had to come up from the south by train—even the cars people drove around.

Actually, Churchill was two communities: the town and the base, a military and research installation about three miles away. The only highway for hundreds of miles in any direction was the little strip of pavement connecting the two. People with vehicles had no alternative but to drive back and forth on that strip. Some of those cars, classics today—Bel Airs, Fairlanes, Plymouths with fins—were really "souped up." But it didn't make much difference. They really had nowhere to go. On Friday nights, bored drivers could only rev them noisily at stop signs. You'd see their red taillights as they headed out to the base, and in about fifteen minutes they'd be back again. Over and over again—it was sad. They were like birds in a cage. Everyone dreamed of the day they would go south again and head out on the Trans-Canada, with nothing but wide-open road and wind in their hair, all the way to the West Coast.

Many gifted women today are like those cars up in Churchill. They were designed for greater things than the restricted opportunities they have been offered. Naturally they chafe. This is not how they were destined to live. And in their hearts they long to become all that they were meant to be. I know a very capable Christian woman for whom doors were consistently closed, until she began to fear that maybe life was passing her by. In her pain she prayed: "God, give me one chance to do my very best." God answered that prayer, which is now framed on her office wall. She drives on the open road now, with the wind in her face, and the world is a better place because of it. This is part of what Jesus came to make possible.

Jesus Upgrades Mary

In his gospel, Luke describes an informal gathering at a home in Bethany, near Jerusalem (Luke 10:38–42). Jesus, the controversial rabbi from Galilee, was visiting, and people were coming and going in a great state of excitement. Stories of miracles followed him wherever he went, while his teaching generated an equal amount of electricity. He appeared intent on turning accepted ideas upside down. He regularly contradicted prevailing wisdom. When the religious establishment told people to zig, Jesus generally advised them to zag. His opponents were infuriated, but the crowds were fascinated. Jesus was a breath of fresh air.

Just as the apostle Paul was trained under the great Pharisee Gamaliel (Acts 22:3), male disciples and devotees pressed close to Jesus and hung on his every word. It was a typical scene for that culture in that day—except for one jarring feature. A woman also was present, sitting, as Luke put it, "at the Lord's feet." A woman! Mary, the sister of Lazarus, was soaking up everything Jesus said, oblivious to the discomfort she was probably creating for some males in the room. These men saw Mary behaving like a rabbinic pupil, a student of the Law. She had overreached her proper station in life. She had no business being there.

Mary's sister Martha was equally distraught. By becoming a student, on an equal footing with men, Mary was neglecting her share of traditional female duties in the kitchen. So Martha came in to complain directly to Jesus. We can imagine the men in the room smiling to themselves, anticipating that Mary's brief presumption was about to end. But Jesus surprised them. He declared that Mary was doing the right thing. And by saying so, he confirmed her right (along with that of women after her) to engage in serious study.[1] He obviously believed she had the capacity for it; he must also have foreseen opportunities for her to put her learning to good use. This little incident, and the whole dossier that it represents, illustrates how the coming of Jesus was the launch of a gender revolution.

The Spirit-Filled Liberator

After growing up as a carpenter's son in the hill town of Nazareth, Jesus asked to be baptized by his cousin John. On that occasion he received an anointing of the Spirit, then was led into the desert for a time of testing and refinement. When he returned, he stood up in the synagogue in his hometown and read from the book of Isaiah these familiar words: "The Spirit of the Lord is on me, because he has anointed me to preach good news to the poor. He has sent me to proclaim freedom for the prisoners and recovery of sight for the blind, to release the oppressed, to proclaim the year of the Lord's favor" (Luke 4:18–19). His concern was for the poor, for prisoners, for the blind and oppressed. With these words Jesus began his ministry and at the same time served notice of his priorities. Like the prophets who had preceded him, Jesus would be empowered by the Spirit and intent on liberating victims of suffering and oppression in its various forms.

Jesus came as a liberator. That is what the title of "savior" means, once its sense is translated into plain speech. It all fits together, then, that his name should be Jesus, the contemporary equivalent to Joshua, which likewise carried the meaning of savior. His mission was to rescue and release humanity from sin and all its evil consequences, from the curse in all its manifestations. He announced that in his person the reign of God had already arrived, and a beachhead had been established for the purpose eventually of completely overthrowing the dominion of darkness. He saw himself binding Satan like a thief might bind a strong homeowner in order to plunder his stuff (Matt. 12:29). He envisioned Satan beginning to fall from his lofty position of earthly dominance and oppression (Luke 10:18).

As John the Evangelist saw things, Jesus was the liberator par excellence. "If the Son sets you free," John recorded, "you will be free indeed" (John 8:36). This was true in a host of ways. Jesus' words of forgiveness liberated souls from the crushing weight of guilt and shame. Through his death and resurrection he struck a fatal blow to the ultimate bondage of death. But the freedom of the Son was not restricted to a realm of "spiritual" blessings, or to an entirely future hope. As a liberator, Jesus tackled the real-world face of oppression. His teaching brought clarity to a world of deceptions. His miracles of healing addressed the suffering of disease and disability. His works of exorcism challenged the demonic powers. And he boldly confronted injustice by denouncing the errors and hypocrisy of the Jewish religious leaders.

Jesus scorned man-made rules and teachings that unfairly burdened and restricted people. He had a special place in his heart for the underdog, seeking out society's cast-offs and drawing the marginalized into the center of the action. He criticized the Pharisees for their love of honor. Instead, he extolled the merits of unsophisticated and powerless children. He called for a servant attitude in anyone aspiring to leadership, and to reinforce his point, wrapped himself in a towel and washed the feet of his disciples.

He challenged the rich to become poor and practiced what he preached by having no place to lay his own head. The kingdom he preached, and inaugurated, was really an "upside-down kingdom,"[2] because it stood established power and authority on its head. In the first century "the poor" were those who lacked standing, influence, and earthly hope. But Jesus promised: "Blessed are you who are poor, for yours is the kingdom of God" (Luke 6:20).

Jesus' response to women was consistent with this overarching theme of liberation. A bold new egalitarian attitude toward women characterized his ministry from the start.[3] Jesus was not just another culturally conditioned first-century Jew, whose attitude and behavior was thoroughly described in the last chapter. He was something different.

For most of us, *this* is the Jesus we never knew. His kingdom did not belong to this age. It did not reflect the patterns of the fallen world. Jesus was about discontinuity more than continuity. He was about the new rather than the old. He warned people that new wine could not be kept safely in old wineskins. Inevitably it would find a way to burst out. How ironic that contemporary followers of this Jesus are so often conservative by temperament, seeking (even desperately at times) to maintain the status quo—the familiar ways in which, it seems, we have always done things.

The Quiet Subversion of Male Privilege

It is true that Jesus never *explicitly* contradicted prevailing assumptions about gender. He never stood up, for example, and announced: "You have heard gender hierarchy preached, but I say unto you that such hierarchy is totally off the mark." Instead, Jesus spoke loudest through his actions and attitudes. He conducted himself in relation to women in ways that were quietly subversive of the status quo. It was not so much what he said, as how he related to women, that was revolutionary. With respect to women "his life style was so remarkable that one can only call it astonishing. He treated women as fully human, equal to men in every respect; no word of deprecation about women, as such, is ever found on his lips."[4]

Language that demeans women was (and still is) pervasive. Even the Old Testament prophets themselves were not untainted by it in their own speech patterns. In predicting God's judgment upon the Egyptians, and their future fear and trembling at God's uplifted hand against them, Isaiah wrote that "the Egyptians will be like women" (Isa. 19:16). Likewise Nahum, in preaching woe against the evil city of Nineveh, scornfully described its defenders this way: "Look at your troops—they are all women!" (Nah. 3:13). To be a woman was to be weak and pathetic.

But this is not the way Jesus spoke. And it is his attitude and behavior that women today, like their female counterparts in first-century Palestine, find so compelling and hopeful. British writer Dorothy Sayers observes, Jesus "never mapped out their sphere for them, never urged them to be feminine or jeered at them for being female."[5] The fact that it was *God incarnate* who modeled such attitudes is especially good news for women.

Jesus' countercultural attitude toward women was also evident in his direct personal encounters with women, and the frequency of them. Women were often the beneficiaries of his miracles of healing, and in many such acts he demonstrated his sensitivity to, and compassion for, women in their plight. His response to a widow who had just lost her only son is a good example (Luke 7:11–17). With similar sensitivity he picked out a struggling widow from the Jerusalem crowd, noted her sacrificial contribution to the temple coffers, and publicly commended her faith and generosity (Mark 12:41–44).

Moreover, Jesus was not afraid of ritual uncleanness when touched by a woman with an issue of blood, but instead engaged her in conversation and healed her chronic condition (Mark 5:25–34). Numerous times in his teaching he drew illustrations and parables from the sphere in which women lived and with which they were most familiar (for example, the parable of the persistent widow in Luke 18:1–8). In the parable of the lowly housewife and her lost coin (Luke 15:8–10), he was bold enough to make the woman in the story represent God.

In contrast to the Old Testament's treatment of divorce, which focuses on a man's rights and responsibilities, Jesus laid out in gender-symmetrical fashion God's expectations of *both* husbands and wives (Mark 10:11–12). Likewise in the account of the woman caught in adultery (John 8:1–11), Jesus appears to have held his male audience accountable for their complicity in similar sins. In contrast to the prevailing strategy for minimizing sexual promiscuity, which was to keep women sequestered and covered, Jesus put his instructional emphasis on men showing self-restraint and abstaining from leering glances and lustful thoughts (Matt. 5:28). Some women were his personal friends. Jesus earned the trust of women. His touch was often healing and always pure. Mary, the sister of Lazarus, felt sufficiently safe with him that she publicly caressed his feet and let down her hair (an action considered risqué for the times) in his presence (John 12:1–8).

The instance in which Jesus most shockingly violated social protocol—even the disciples were taken aback by his actions—was his encounter with the Samaritan woman (John 4), an individual with three strikes against her: she was a Samaritan, a sinner, and a woman. He didn't backpedal from her in fear. A few years ago the leader of a Christian organization fired his secretary, despite her modest deportment, because *he* was having lustful thoughts about *her*! Shouldn't he have fired himself instead? In any event, Jesus would never have felt the need to push the woman away like that. He decisively relinquished in advance any sexual possibilities with the woman, and so was freed up to relate to her as a person.

There is no hint of disdain in Jesus' comments to her, despite the fact that he was uncannily familiar with her sinful past and reputation. He risked his own reputation in order to have a meaningful conversation with her. He did not patronize her, but engaged her in a serious theological dialogue despite her relative lack of religious education.

This was a far cry from the rabbinic advice that it was an ill-advised waste of time for Jewish men to talk at any length with women because of their abysmal ignorance.[6] There was no apparent reason why he should have had any interest in her. That he evidently did she found remarkable. Empowered with one of the earliest disclosures of Jesus' messianic identity, the woman ran back to her community as one of the New Testament's first missionaries. The treatment she received from him transformed her.

Taking all of this together, is it any wonder that women were drawn to Jesus and became so loyal to him? They recognized his teaching and example for the good news it really was, and not least as good news for them *as women*.

Female Followers and Witnesses

Jesus selected men for his inner circle of twelve disciples, which some suggest sent a message that church leaders should always be male. Actually, there is good evidence that the disciples were chosen to parallel the heads of the twelve tribes of Israel. The message in such symbolism was that Jesus was inaugurating a *new* Israel, *not* that this new

Israel, the church, needed to be patriarchal like the old one. (Jesus' consistently positive treatment of women in the gospel narratives is a more reliable indicator of his heart attitude on this matter.) His selection of male disciples was also a practical accommodation to the realities of first-century Palestinian life. For example, it would have more than raised eyebrows if Jesus' itinerant band of disciples, who often found themselves without proper nighttime accommodation, had included disciples of the opposite sex. A public perception of impropriety would have been almost impossible to refute.

Nonetheless it is remarkable how quickly Jesus gathered around him a cohort of female followers, and how closely and tenaciously they appear to have kept up with his itinerary. Scandalously enough by the standards of that day, they actually traveled with him. The membership of this group began to form during Jesus' Galilean ministry and included a number of affluent women who supported his ministry in practical and financial ways (Luke 8:1–3). Some years later, when it became evident that Jesus was doomed to Roman crucifixion, the reactions of his male and female followers diverged significantly. The male disciples, we are told, deserted him and fled in panic for their lives (Matt. 26:56). The women stuck by him and were faithful.

They did not conceal their emotions as they followed him along the Via Dolorosa, and positioned themselves close enough to speak with him as he passed. They were the last to leave the cross and the first to discover the empty tomb. What all this amounts to is this: Jesus had essentially two groups of followers who interacted with one another but remained distinguished along gender lines. This arrangement was as close to Jesus' own ideal of gender mutuality as the cultural protocols of the day would allow. Even so, it was a remarkable and unprecedented gesture of inclusion. As New Testament scholar Joachim Jeremias observes, "Jesus knowingly overthrew custom when he allowed women to follow him."[7]

Jesus spoke some of his most powerful words to women. To Martha, Jesus proclaimed, "I am the resurrection and the life" (John 11:25). He thus supported women as intelligent enough to deal with such a weighty proclamation and trustworthy enough to relay that information to others. Likewise we should not underestimate the significance of the fact that women were privileged to be the first witnesses of the resurrection of Jesus (Mark 16), despite the lesser value patriarchal society attached to the formal testimony of women. Proclamation of the resurrection was the distinguishing feature of the apostolic gospel and the very heart of the early church's apologetic. Yet it was a history-altering reality to which the attention of the apostles was first brought by women. From a cultural perspective, the irony and affirmation in all of this was huge.

Not surprisingly, those waiting and praying in the upper room for the promised coming of the Holy Spirit included "the women" (Acts 1:14) among the group of about one hundred and twenty (v. 15). Some English translations of verse 16 still have Peter addressing only the "brothers," but we have a pretty good indication from the previous verses that he did not use the term *adelphoi* here in a gender-exclusive sense. Women were full participants in those momentous events, and Pentecost was a further vindication of their central role in the kingdom of God. Tongues of fire came upon each of them, and "all" (surely including the women) were filled with the Holy Spirit (2:3–4). The Spirit was distributed to everyone in such a nondiscriminatory way that it brought to Peter's mind a prophecy of Joel: "I will pour out my Spirit on all people. Your sons and daughters will prophesy . . . both men and women" (Acts 2:17–18). This was the strongest expression yet of the trajectory of the Spirit, and it clarified where Jesus' heart had been on the matter all along.

Jesus and the Gospel Writers

The egalitarian vision of Jesus was appreciated to different degrees by the four gospel writers. Of all the evangelists, Luke seems to have best grasped and celebrated this side of Jesus and was most in tune with this aspect of the trajectory of the Spirit.[8] There is considerable evidence, first of all, to support the theory that Mary, the mother of Jesus, was a significant information source for Luke. The narratives of Jesus' birth (Luke 1–2) are unique to Luke and reflect Mary's perspective. She is not a silent icon, as in Matthew, but psychologically real and even feisty (just read her song, the Magnificat, in Luke 1 for conclusive proof of this). Eliza-beth, Mary's cousin, and Anna the prophetess also figure largely in the infancy story. All three speak out prophetically too, lending further stature to their profiles. By contrast, Joseph and, to a lesser extent the muted Zechariah, function as quiet support cast for the women. Is it pos-sible that Luke is engaging deliberately in a bit of role reversal here?

In numerous small ways, Luke presses for a deeper appreciation of Jesus' egalitarian spirit. Luke's outlook is apparent in how he chooses to edit material common to the synoptic gospel writers. What he adds and what he leaves out, as he handles these shared resources, reflects his unique sensitivity and interests. The sinful woman who anoints Jesus is given an extended affirmation (7:36–50). Luke mentions in passing that Jesus' friend Martha is the head of her home (10:38). The entourage of women following Jesus show up earlier, and they have a more human face when they do. They actually have names—Mary (aka Magdalene), Joanna, and Susanna (8:1–3). And they are shown to have made a more significant contribution to his ministry. Luke reports that "these women were helping to support them out of their own means" (v. 3). They were more than camp cooks and bottle-washers.

Matthew and Mark note that the women did not return to the tomb until after the Sabbath, but only Luke takes the opportunity also to commend them for their righteous observance of the day of rest (23:56). While Matthew notes only that they returned to the tomb to investigate, Luke underscores that they were on a mission of mercy and human dig-nity. These women were subsequently greeted with skepticism when they reported their findings to the disciples (24:11), and the reader is left to wonder whether this reaction was due entirely to the preposter-ousness of their report, or whether a sexist attitude on the part of the disciples can also be detected. Luke records an almost identical reaction when the female servant Rhoda later excitedly reported that the recently imprisoned Peter was standing on the doorstep (Acts 12:12–16).

Beyond all this, there was a deliberate attempt on Luke's part to create a kind of gender symmetry in the characters he selected for inclusion in his gospel. One thinks of Mary and Joseph, of course, and Zechariah and Elizabeth, but also Simeon and Anna. Later on in Acts,

Luke continues the pattern with Ananias and Sapphira, Felix and Drusilla, and Priscilla and Aquila. Likewise in Luke's writing a parable about a woman is often followed by one about a man, and vice versa. By deliberately arranging his material this way, Luke was saying that "man and woman stand together and side by side before God. They are equal in honor and grace; they are endowed with the same gifts and have the same responsibilities."9

Not surprisingly, Luke, more than either Matthew or Mark, stressed the work of the Holy Spirit—so much so, in fact, that Luke's theology has been described as a charismatic theology.10 The biblical links already established between the Spirit and liberating egalitarianism continue to develop here. Jesus' egalitarianism was not emphasized equally by the gospel writers. While each wrote truthfully and under inspiration, and each contributed an important perspective on Jesus, the fact remains, for example, that Matthew saw the ministry of Jesus through a lens still somewhat colored by a patriarchal Jewish worldview. According to Matthew, the holy family received divine guidance through dream messages received by Joseph, while Mary stood by as his demure spouse. Matthew presents ethical material with a male readership in view. For example, a power-grabbing proposal by disciples James and John is presented to Jesus by their mother (Matt. 20:20), while Mark puts the blame squarely on the shoulders of the ambitious men themselves (Mark 10:35–45).

Examples and comparisons of this nature abound. Matthew's more limited appreciation for the gender implications of the gospel of Jesus in no way distorts the truths he mediated to the Christian community. Matthew's blinders were part of the humanness through which God allowed the gospel to be infallibly expressed. The fact that the gospel writers themselves had different levels of insight into Jesus' vision for gender relations helps prepare us for the reality that not all Christians have recognized and embraced this aspect of the Savior's ministry equally.

The Gentleness of God

Every religious revolution involves a transformed and transforming view of God. One of the important things Jesus did was alter humanity's perception of God. The religion of the Jews, with which Jesus identi-fied, was distinguished by a commitment to ethical monotheism—that is, to the worship of a sole personal deity (that's the *mono*-theistic part) who cares about right and wrong (that's why it is called *ethical*). The essence of this God's being was shrouded in glorious radiance and mys-tery, and even the name by which God chose to be known—Yahweh—was enigmatic.

This God was Israel's great champion and warrior. He was frighten-ing in his wrath and awesome when he spoke. He was much greater than any local tribal deity. He ruled the universe and sat in sovereign majesty over the affairs of the nations. Little wonder then, that most of the pro-nouns, word pictures, and analogies Jewish people employed to depict their God were male in orientation. How in those days could anyone of might and authority be conceptualized otherwise? God's characteristics were indelibly associated in the Jewish mind with those of a male leader.

Jesus never questioned the core of Israel's religious understanding. He unequivocally affirmed that God was one and holy. Jesus' innova-tion lay rather in referring to Israel's God as *Father*—a term drawn from the sphere of affectionate family intimacy and security. Jesus used this designation for God when he taught his disciples to pray, and repeated it often in his great ethical manifesto, the Sermon on the Mount (Matt. 5–7). It pervades the Gospels.

It was not as though this term *Father* and the concept it signified was completely missing from the Old Testament. It was not something brand new. But what Jesus did was upgrade this relatively neglected concept of God to center stage. It was his way of counteracting a flawed perception of God that had grown up through the centuries—a per-ception that God was more than anything else aloof, demanding, and punitive. It was never Jesus' intention to suggest that maleness or male-likeness inheres in God's nature. Jesus chose the name Father to under-score the loving, tender, accessible character of God. It was meant to signal an *analogy* between the heart of God and the affection and responsibility human parents feel toward their children.

Jesus left a legacy that henceforth believers thought about God in this newer, familial way. This in itself already challenged the traditional

patriarchal mind-set, for it called people to reconceptualize their relationship to God less in terms of rigid vertical authority, and more in
terms of relational intimacy and freedom. The sovereign Lord over all
had now become *Abba* (Mark 14:36).

The Myth of God's Maleness

It gradually dawned on Jesus' followers that he was more than the Mes- ?
siah, more than the promised great deliverer of God's people. He was
God incarnate, God present with us in human form. This understanding of Jesus is most pronounced in the writings of the apostle John, but
it is also present elsewhere in the New Testament. In time, the early
church became convinced that this belief was essential to the logic of
salvation and to the gospel message itself. If Jesus was God, then he
must have existed from all eternity. He could not have had his beginning
when Mary conceived him, or indeed at any point in time. Eternity is,
after all, an essential attribute of deity, so there could never have been
a time when he was not. Prior to his physical advent as Mary's baby,
then, the Son coexisted eternally with the Father and the Spirit.

Ever since then, Christians have used male language to designate
two of the three persons of the Godhead—the Father and the Son. That
means that male descriptors are in the majority. Unfortunately, as some
feminists correctly observe, this terminology has led to some deeply
entrenched misunderstandings of God's nature. Once an image of God
is established in the mind, whether it is Baal, Thor, or Allah, it becomes
a symbol of what is most valuable and most worthy of respect and imi-
tation. It comes in this way to exert a tremendous influence on people.

This led feminist Mary Daly to famously complain that "if God is
male, then the male is God."[11] In a sense she was right. If the church
ascribes maleness to God, we can expect the church to prioritize male
attributes over female and to privilege men over women. The church
will not be able to help itself, for we instinctively attach greater honor
to those things we believe are closest to the way God is.

By way of response, we must insist that there is nothing especially
male about God. As Genesis made clear, men and women reflect God's
likeness equally (see chapter 3). Neither sex is a preferred or privileged

reflection of God's nature. God is no more like a man than a woman. The biblical imagery of Father and Son has been a stumbling block to Muslims for fourteen centuries. They cannot get past a crudely literal apprehension of this relationship and postulate that Christians must hold that God the Father had sexual relations with Mary to beget a son. This, of course, they find blasphemous and respond by denying that the prophet Jesus is the Son of God. According to the Koran, "Those who say: 'The Lord of Mercy has begotten a son,' preach a monstrous falsehood, at which the very heavens might crack, the earth break asunder, and the mountains crumble to dust."[12]

Most Christians regard such Islamic confusion as naive. But many Christians stumble on a different reading of the biblical descriptions of the persons of the Godhead. Just as Muslim theology cannot conceptualize the Father and the Son without the one procreating the other, so many literalist Christians cannot conceive of God the Father or God the Son without the two possessing actual maleness. The only way forward is to really get hold of the fact that God's true nature transcends our conceptual and linguistic capabilities and to stress the difference between literal and analogical terminology. Father and Son are *analogical* terms. They mean that the first two persons of the Trinity, in some limited ways, relate to one another *like* a human father and a son might relate. For the church to move on from its patriarchal past, it must understand that Father and Son are terms designed to witness to the shared nature and intimate love relationship between the two persons.

The Word Became Flesh

Even after this is all sorted out, the fact remains that the Son, the second person of the eternal Trinity, came to earth as a man. Since his purpose was to become human, he had basically two options: come as a man or come as a woman. Arriving in some androgynous earth-suit might look like the perfect compromise, but it would not have been a *real* incarnation—he would not have really been one of us. The fancy name for this unavoidable reality is "the scandal of particularity." It means that no matter what form the incarnation takes, one side or the other is likely to complain.

Still, there is the nagging question of whether there might have been something more fitting or suitable about the incarnation of divinity in a male form, as opposed to a female. Fortunately, this is a question which the apostle John has already addressed. He taught that the incarnation was the historical moment in which divinity became *enfleshed*: "The Word became flesh," he declared (John 1:14). In other words, God did not take upon himself mere maleness (or singleness, or Jewishness, either). With a much larger and more welcoming embrace, he took upon himself our *full* humanity in all its racial, marital, and gendered diversity. The things he achieved as our representative generated benefits available to men and women alike, for we all belong to one and the same flesh. God became human. God became an earthling. "What distinguishes Jesus as normative is not his maleness but the quality of his humanness."[13] The specific gender form of his incarnation is never treated in Scripture as theologically significant at all. It should not matter to us either.

What to Do with Names for God

One of the important theological challenges of our time is to decide what to do with the God-titles we have learned from Jesus. To try to compensate for the perception of maleness in the Christian God by venerating Mary, or by promoting the Holy Spirit as a feminine deity, are efforts doomed to slim gains and ultimate futility. Some have called for a replacement of all masculine imagery and pronouns with neutral alternatives, but one of the weaknesses of this strategy (at least in English) is that the *personal* nature of God tends to get eclipsed when impersonal imagery is used. God is far more than a force or influence. He is a personal being, who speaks and listens and responds and feels deeply. No solution to the gender problem is worth it if it obscures this truth.

An alternative proposal is to try to put male and female images of God on an equal footing. In this way, it is hoped, gender-biased perceptions of God will not develop. But this proposal has problems as well. We have no natural analogs to a personal being who is sometimes male and sometimes female. To employ language in a way which suggests that God perpetually oscillates in his identity could easily make

God seem schizophrenic and strange—a confusing deity with an air of unreality about him.

The best solution is to continue using biblical descriptors for God, but to be much more careful to ensure that they are no longer interpreted in immature, unthinking ways. This will ensure that the worship language of the contemporary church remains in continuity with that of Christians through the ages. Imperiled as it is by fads and shallowness, the church today needs to remain in solidarity with twenty centuries of faithful believers, and this is one good way to do it. But the classic Christian names for God must be used with an enlightened awareness of their conceptual limitations. Christians must be delivered from the mistaken practice of idolizing a male deity.

What Are the Greater Things to Come?

Jesus' brief ministry on earth was powerful, radical, and at times spectacular. Toward the end of this time, Jesus predicted that his disciples would do "even greater things" than he had done (John 14:12). In what sense did he mean greater? Did he mean that they would be able to perform even more stunningly supernatural signs and wonders than Jesus himself had done? The record of church history tends not to support this conjecture. Did he perhaps mean that the church, in terms of cumulative statistics, would evangelize more extensively and perform more service through multiple millennia than Jesus had by himself during his brief lifetime? Partly, perhaps, but by itself this point seems too obvious to be *all* that Jesus was saying. Likely he also meant that believers would *extend the trajectory* of his ministry further along, as they worked out the implications of the principles he introduced.[14] As Sue Monk Kidd has so beautifully suggested, discovering and developing "the mind of Christ" (1 Cor. 2:16) inevitably puts us on a "bending, curving journey toward the light."[15]

In 1939, Bill Hewlett and Dave Packard, two young engineers out of Stanford University, started a little electronics business in their garage in Palo Alto, California. They were creative guys with an entrepreneurial bent, and before long Hewlett-Packard was a going concern. The company was always on the cutting edge of electronics and computing and grew exponentially. At least as significant as its technological genius was its innovative management style, which includes now-famous concepts like "management by walking around," management by objectives, the open-door policy, and flex-hours. A book outlining their corporate values, *The HP-Way* (1995), has had enormous influence.

By the time the founders died (Dave in 1996 and Bill in 2001), the company was an international giant doing over $40 billion in annual business. Today, HP continues to press ahead into new technologies that even Hewlett and Packard themselves could scarcely have imagined. Its corporate motto—"Invent"—is part of the founders' enduring legacy, as is a corporate ethos that perpetuates their groundbreaking respect for employees as team members. Today, as the company does ever greater things, it extends the trajectory of what two guys began with just $500 in capital in a garage behind their house. Bill and Dave's vision lives on.

Jesus had sown revolutionary seeds. The church would subsequently nurture many of them into full and mature plants. Before long, as we know, the church took the gospel far beyond the Jewish cocoon in which it had begun its life. Ultimately, the church is destined to overcome gender hierarchy and oppression. If the followers of Jesus are to fill up what is still lacking in his *sufferings* (Col. 1:24), as Scripture indicates, is it not reasonable to expect them to carry forward to greater fulfillment the *liberation program* Jesus has already set in motion? To assist in achieving such "greater things," Christ has promised the church his Spirit, who will guide us into all truth (John 16:13).

. . . .

CHAPTER SUMMARY

Jesus, the Spirit-filled liberator and supreme revealer of God's will and ways, inaugurated a new attitude toward women and established patterns of respect toward them that were unprecedented in his time. He indicated in this way the direction the Spirit was headed in the redemptive task of restoring the original pattern of equality, freedom, and mutuality in gender relations. The work of transforming gender dynamics was not completed by Jesus during his brief sojourn on earth, but the seeds of the new pattern—the kingdom way—were sown then, and these were destined to bear more fruit in the years ahead.

wrong - completed while on earth.

Questions for Individual or Group Reflection

1. What was quietly revolutionary about Jesus' approach to women?

2. Share something you find appealing or disturbing about Jesus' behavior toward women.

3. What significance, if any, do you see in women being the first witnesses to the resurrection?

4. How should we interpret the biblical terminology of "Father" and "Son"? Is God more like a man than a woman? Why do you believe as you do?

5. What is there about Jesus' view of God that helps undermine patriarchy?

6. Jesus affirmed women without being offensive. How can we imitate his example?

CHAPTER 7

Gender in the Early Church

SUBSTANTIAL PROGRESS TOWARD GOSPEL IDEALS

When surfing conditions are near perfect, excitement builds up and down our California coast, from Sunset Cliffs to San Onofre. Then even some seminary students head out with their boards loaded, their windows down, and their music loud. They take the freeway and park as close to the coast as they can. They run into the surf, get prone on their boards, and start paddling into deeper water.

During lulls between sets of waves they'll wait around in pods like orcas. But when a really cool wave is sighted, a murmur of anticipation moves through the group. They start positioning themselves to make the most of the coming wall of water. You don't fight waves like these, especially the big ones that have been building from Japan. You catch them, and you go with *their* flow.

The well-tanned, seasoned veterans know the precise angle and moment at which to commit. In a second, they're up on all fours, then on their feet and flying along with the roaring wave at their shoulder. Their balance is incredible—humanity and nature in exquisite tension—and they keep it going, and going, and going. Sometimes they will even run a spent wave right into shallow water, stepping off with casual elegance. They may stand there for a fleeting moment of triumph. Then they're off again into the deeper water for more. I can understand when some say that there's nothing quite like it in the whole world.

The early church caught the wave of the Spirit, and it took them for quite a ride too. The earthly ministry of Jesus was the great leap forward in the Spirit-guided movement to restore the original gender pattern of equality and freedom. What Christ began, the church was destined to continue and develop. This resulted in very empowering new practices and some radically countercultural ways of relating between men and women. In a later chapter we will note how some patriarchal thinking and attitudes also persisted in the early Christian community, and to some extent in the minds of the biblical authors themselves. But we begin by acknowledging and celebrating the early church's substantial progress toward gospel ideals, a progress stimulated by the gender-equalizing impact of Pentecost.

The Gender-Equalizing Impact of Pentecost

The day of Pentecost, immediately following the resurrection of Jesus, marked the launch of the church as the new people of God. At that point in time, which coincided with a Jewish festival commemorating the giving of the Law at Sinai, God poured out his Spirit—the Spirit of Christ—for the express purpose of creating something new. The church was the *new* chosen people, the *new* royal priesthood, the *new* holy nation, the *new* people belonging to God (1 Peter 2:9). The revised New Testament definition of a true Jew was no longer one who was circumcised outwardly and physically, but one who was circumcised inwardly by the Spirit, and thereby set apart for God and his purposes (Rom. 2:28–29). From now on, this is what it would mean to be "Abraham's seed" and an heir to God's promises to his chosen ones (Gal. 3:29).

Moreover, this new people of God were to be a kind of new temple, replacing the old edifice in Jerusalem. God's Spirit now dwelt in *it* in a special way (Eph. 2:21–22). Bricks and mortar were superceded by "living stones"—actual living, breathing persons. The edifice on Jerusalem's temple mount had given way to a globally networked human community. The presence of the Holy Spirit was more intense within this new assembly, this new *ecclesia*, than outside of it. Consequently, there was greater liberty inside it for the Spirit to heal, restore, and recreate human relationships to better mirror God's inner life. The church did not exist just to get the gospel message out in words. It was also to be a prototype of the kingdom, a city set on a hill that modeled to the world what the future was eventually going to look like. The church was to be a countercultural alternative to the way human society functioned. It could not be different simply by resolving to be so, but because the empowering Spirit of God was actively present within it.

As mentioned in chapter 6, it is significant that when the promised Spirit came in Pentecostal fullness, he came upon a gender-diverse group (Acts 1:14). Not just men, those assumed by existing social conventions to be qualified to lead, were affected. *Both* men and women, Luke pointedly observed, were filled with the Spirit, as tongues of fire came to rest upon each of them (Acts 2:3). The early Christian community recognized this dramatic event as a fulfillment of a prophecy of Joel 2:28–29, a prophecy that powerfully reinforced the gender-inclusive character of the Spirit's outpouring:

> In the last days, God says,
> I will pour out my Spirit on *all people*.
> Your sons *and daughters* will prophesy,
> Your young men will see visions,
> Your old men will dream dreams.
> Even on my servants, *both men and women*,
> I will pour out my Spirit in those days,
> And they will prophesy. (Acts 2:17–18, my emphasis)

Joel's prophecy underscores the generous and inclusive scope of the Spirit's outpouring. It is not only age-inclusive, but gender-inclusive as well. It describes an indiscriminate deluging of Spirit power on women and men alike. At this point the burden of proof shifts to those who wish to argue that Christian service in the power of the Spirit should continue to conform to traditional gender protocols.

The same thing held true in later New Testament descriptions of the gifts (*charismata*) of the Spirit. The two main lists of such spiritual gifts are found in Romans 12 and 1 Corinthians 12. These gift-lists, which are representative rather than exhaustive, mention abilities granted to individual believers for building up others and the body of

Christ as a whole. They were meant for ministry, and responsibility came along with receiving them. In other words, they were intended to be developed and *used*, for the health of the whole body depended on the active contribution of each gifted member.

Spiritual gifts were not apportioned according to gender, and their use was not to be restricted by gender. In fact, it is impossible to predict how, and to whom, the Spirit will distribute gifts among believers, because the Holy Spirit distributes them "just as he determines" (1 Cor. 12:11). If the distribution was conditional in any way upon gender, the granting of particular forms of *charismata* would, to that extent at least, be predictable. It would follow gender lines. But Paul insists that God's sovereign decision is entirely "as he wills," not according to preestablished rules or foreseeable limitations. Thus, Spirit-filled and Spirit-gifted women are to be involved alongside men in the use of their gifts for Christian ministry.

It is not surprising at all, therefore, to find women validated by the apostle Paul as they prayed and prophesied in the early church's public worship times (1 Cor. 11:5). This is exactly what the prophet Joel predicted would happen, and this is what had already taken place at Pentecost. And it is important to understand that prophecy involved far more than periodic ecstatic utterances or occasional supernatural predictions of the future. Prophecy denoted Spirit-empowered proclamation and authoritative teaching.

The Inclusive Practices of the Early Church

Later on in the book of Acts, Luke noted that four daughters of the deacon Philip were renowned in the early church for their prophetic gifts (Acts 21:9). If this was inappropriate behavior, Luke should have said so and pointed out that Philip's leadership credentials were suspect, since he was failing to manage his household well (1 Tim. 3:4). As an anointed pronouncement of an authoritative word from God, prophecy was certainly a prominent spiritual gift. If its exercise was permitted of women, and we know from 1 Corinthians 11:5 that it was, it is hard to imagine that the church would prohibit women from exercising other "lesser" gifts, such as administration and teaching.

Moreover, the apostle Paul instructed the Corinthian believers that when they came together to worship as *adelphoi*, they were each to contribute out of their unique personal giftedness to the common good (1 Cor. 14:26). Their contributions, Paul explained, might take the form of a word of instruction, a revelation, a tongue, or the like. An important question is whether in this context *adelphoi* designates "brothers" (in which case the public exercise of gifts in view was restricted to men) or "brothers and sisters" (in which case both men and women were being invited to use their gifts in gender-mixed public settings). As New Testament scholar Mark Strauss has pointed out, "the Greek masculine noun *adelphos* can carry the sense of a physical 'brother,' but in the New Testament is more often used figuratively of the kinship between believers."[1]

Traditionally, Christians in the English-speaking world have followed the King James Version in restricting this to brothers (that is, to males only). But the translators of other more recent English-language versions have concluded that Paul had *both* women and men in view when he chose this term. Given the extensive involvement of women in Paul's church-planting and missionary ventures, it is difficult to believe that he intended *adelphoi* to be taken in the less common and more restricted male sense. It seems more plausible that he used it in the inclusive sense, just as he did elsewhere, for example, in his call for Christian consecration: "I urge you, *adelphoi*, in view of God's mercy, to offer your bodies as living sacrifices" (Rom. 12:1). The implication of this interpretation of 1 Corinthians 14:26 is obvious: the gifts of the Spirit were not only to be received, but also exercised, without regard to artificially imposed gender restrictions. When we remember that the Corinthian women were already prophesying and praying in public, this gender-inclusive assessment of the Corinthian church dynamic seems pretty conclusive.

What Did "Neither Male nor Female" Mean?

Nowhere in the entire New Testament is the gospel of freedom in Christ proclaimed more vigorously than in the epistle to the Galatians. This little manifesto was prompted by the apostle Paul's fear that "a different gospel"—a legalistic threat that was in fact no gospel at all—might be embraced by the Christian community in Galatia. Paul's thesis was that, in Christ, believers had been freed from any obligation to continue observing Jewish customs. As a result, observant Jews had no religious advantage or privileged status over uncircumcised Gentiles in the new Christian community. All believers were now children of God through faith in Christ (Gal. 3:26). All enjoyed the unconditionally accepting embrace of the Father because they were equally "clothed" with Christ (v. 27). The old two-tiered religious system based on Jewish privilege had been dismantled.

But that was not all. Not only the religious and ethnic distinctions Paul had been considering up to this point (between Jews and Greeks), but also the social distinctions (between slaves and free) and gender distinctions (between men and women) were reduced to irrelevance in the new unity of Christian fellowship. "You are all one in Christ Jesus" (Gal. 3:28). It is not perfectly clear why Paul took these sideways swipes at prejudice against slaves and women, since up to this point their concerns were not center-stage. It is very possible that he was fed up with the sort of arrogance fostered by a common synagogue prayer, in which Jewish men thanked God they were not born Gentile, slave, or female.[2] As noted earlier in this book, such a threefold prejudice was widespread in both pagan and Jewish circles. Paul attacked this old prejudice to point out, in the boldest terms possible, how radical and far-reaching were the implications of the gospel.

The phrase "neither male nor female" is widely regarded as the high-water mark of the apostle Paul's views on gender. It is a clear statement of Paul's egalitarian viewpoint, of what he believed most passionately, and what he was finally able to express without any accommodation to patriarchal premises. Critics of this interpretation argue that Paul simply meant that Jews and Gentiles, slaves and free, men and women, all had *access to salvation* through faith in Christ. They argue that the passage really says nothing to discredit the perpetuation of other proper and legitimate distinctions between the various groupings, including stratified roles for men and women. They believe that gender hierarchy is eminently compatible with the "spiritual equality" affirmed here.

Such a restrictive interpretation is incorrect. First of all, the nonenslaved Jewish males' prayer of gratitude did not assume that Gentiles, slaves, and women were categorically cut off from any hope of salvation. It assumed instead that these categories of persons were inferior and disadvantaged. It is significant that where this three-part prayer is mentioned in the Jewish Talmud, the concern is for restricting their full participation in the *educational and worship activities* of the Jewish religion.[3] Access to salvation by slaves and women was never questioned in the early church either. That was assumed. Paul's remark would have been strangely superfluous if he only had access to forgiveness of sins in mind. He would have been stating the obvious and wasting his readers' time. It makes a great deal more sense to conclude that Paul was rejecting any privileged treatment or discriminatory practices within the church fellowship, whether those are based on ethnicity, social status, or gender.

Second, Paul did not say that all can be saved through Christ. He says that all of these groups are one in Christ Jesus. It makes most sense to interpret the oneness he speaks of as a unity of equality and mutual dignity. The countercultural community of God was to treat as transparent the ethnic, social, and gender differences so evident and important in the pagan world. Every Christian was, so to speak, now wearing the same uniform: they were all clothed with Christ. Gentiles, slaves, and women were not to be treated as second-class citizens of the kingdom.

In the case of gender distinctions, Paul meant that they were now irrelevant to the structuring of Christian social life. The church was not to ignore sexual differences, but these were never again to be a basis for assigning privileges or imposing restrictions. Women were no longer to be dismissed as dumber, morally weaker, or more dangerous than men. They were not to be prevented from assuming roles of responsibility on the basis of their sex. They were no longer expected to act in obsequious ways and to leave the important decision-making to men.

Third, Paul declared this gender-transparent oneness in Christ in the context of an overarching declaration of the liberty found through the gospel. Before coming to this faith, Paul described people as in custody and locked up (Gal. 3:23). He compared their condition to that of slaves and minors, who chafed under the control of guardians and trustees who were over them. It was all part of a vast system of oppressive principalities and powers (4:1–3), an experience of enslavement (vv. 8–9). But in Christ there was now release, redemption, and liberation from it all. The gospel was about a glorious new freedom. "It is for freedom that Christ has set us free. Stand firm, then, and do not let yourselves be burdened again by a yoke of slavery" (5:1).

Paul's primary foil was the oppressive burden of Jewish legalism. But he sees equally pernicious dynamics in slavery and the social patterns of gender oppression, and declares a gospel of freedom from all of them. It was not without cause that he described the liberating Christ as himself "born of a woman" (Gal. 4:4). Paul's point was that womankind had been graciously granted a role in achieving humanity's salvation and allowed to participate in her liberation from the judgment of the fall.

Hopefully it is clear by now that Paul's manifesto of liberation in Galatians 3:28 was about more than women's access to forgiveness of sins through Christ and the assurance of eternal life. One final consideration reinforces such a conclusion, and it is this: the salvation proclaimed in the New Testament was never a purely "spiritual" or disembodied hope for the life to come. It was a gospel that was to become incarnate in the social structures of the real world and to transform what it touched. The disciples had been taught to pray that God's will be done on earth as it was in heaven. Since through Christ women were now equal to men in spiritual things (heavenly matters), the principle of their complete liberation needed also to find expression in their earthly relationships. And the place where this was to begin was in the church itself.[4]

Our friends Tim and Diana are pioneer missionaries to the Nakui (pronounced *nok-we*), an animist people in the remote jungle of northeastern Papua New Guinea. Life has never been easy for the Nakui, and it can be particularly oppressive for their women. The hunt for food never ends, especially the quest for high-protein meat. Finding and killing one of the large water snakes native to the region is always cause for village celebration. Traditionally, however, only men could enjoy this delicacy. Women were not allowed to eat the snake's highly valued meat.

Recently a Nakui man who had become a Christian shocked his community at one of the snake barbecues. He did something unprecedented in that culture. Through new eyes he looked over at his wife and then offered her a share of his portion of roasted snake. She gladly accepted it! It is such a small beginning—such a baby step, really. Nonetheless, it signals early movement in the right direction. It is another sure sign that the Holy Spirit is present and active in Nakui culture.

Are Women Weaker?

The New Testament community, under the spiritual leadership of the apostles, was aware of the gender-equalizing tendencies of the Holy Spirit within it, and understood that the old distinctions of power and privilege were no longer significant in the new thing Christ was creating. Early Christians lived in societies in which these old patterns of privilege remained entrenched, however, and they were conscious of the contrast between the existing social order and the way things were to be in Christ. The apostle Peter was keenly aware of women's social disadvantage in the larger world, but also aware that their subordinate position was a temporary problem rather than a permanent destiny. Conscious of Christian women's equal status in God's eyes, Peter advised Christian husbands: "Live with your wives in an insightful way, showing respect to them as less empowered ones who are actually equal heirs with you of the gracious gift of life, so that nothing will hinder your prayers" (1 Peter 3:7, my translation).

How ironic that Peter's liberating admonition has traditionally been taken as a put-down on women! For centuries the faith and practice of the English-speaking church has been shaped by the King James Version. According to this classic translation, a husband is to give honor to his wife as "the weaker vessel." As a result, the concept of the female as the "weaker vessel" has been branded deep in the consciousness of English-speaking Christians. Alternative renditions as "the weaker sex" (RSV) and "weaker partner" (NIV) have continued the perception that women are defective. This has perpetuated a tremendous amount of stereotyping of women. Too many male Christians have enjoyed speculating on whether the weakness in view here is muscular, emotional, mental, or moral, or perhaps some combination of all of these. Few translations of Scripture have been more hurtful to the dignity of women.

Women's Temporary Social Disadvantage

Christians need to interpret this statement correctly. Note that Peter begins by encouraging husbands, literally, to "cohabit according to knowledge." The NIV translates this phrase "be considerate as you live with your wives." This has led readers to all sorts of patronizing attitudes and sexist jokes, suggesting that men should try to gloss over the multitude of ways in which women are inferior and even irritating. As the NASB so cruelly puts it, a man is to overlook these faults in his spouse, "since she is a woman."

But in fact this text does not call men to be considerate. Rather, it urges them to be *perceptive*. Of all the English translations, the KJV actually wins out here when it reads: "Dwell with them according to knowledge." And what is it of which the savvy husband is supposed to be knowledgeable? Simply this: that despite her inferior status and diminished privilege in society, his wife is his equal in the eyes of God (an equal heir). The way he cohabits with her ought to reflect this uniquely Christian insider information. It will certainly involve being considerate, but a consideration rooted in the knowledge that society does not treat his wife (nor women generally) as they really deserve.

Consider next the phrase describing the wife or the woman, a phrase which the King James Version rendered as "the weaker vessel." In the original Greek text, the crucial word in the phrase is the adjective *asthenestero*, which has almost always been translated as "weaker." This has been inappropriate, unfortunate—even catastrophic. The

Greek root has a semantic range that extends well beyond weaker to include sick, ill, and—most significantly—*powerless*.[5] Of these various options, it appears that the latter—powerlessness—is in mind here. This choice of "powerless" involves no stretching of the facts, for the identical root word is translated "powerless" in Romans 5:6, which reads: "When we were still powerless, Christ died for the ungodly."

It is actually woman's lesser *social* power that is in view. Certainly the word, as it is used elsewhere in Scripture, allows for this possibility, as when Scripture says that "God chose the weak things (*asthene*) of the world to shame the strong. He chose the lowly things of this world and the despised things—and the things that are not—to nullify the things that are" (1 Cor. 1:27–28). Patristic usage is likewise supportive. Yet perhaps the weightiest consideration in favor of interpreting the term this way is that it fits with the overall theme of the epistle. That theme is how to live, without fear or intimidation, as foreigners and strangers in a hostile host culture (1 Peter 2:11)—to live, as it has been recently stated, as resident aliens.[6] Peter writes to oppressed and marginalized people experiencing discrimination. They were, in a social sense, relatively powerless.[7] The burden of proof, in other words, lies with those who would want to interpret the phrase in terms of female physiology or rational ability. In summary, the apostle Peter is suggesting that the woman (or wife) is, in the contemporary idiom, "the less empowered one."

In her book *Good News for Women*, Rebecca Groothuis agrees that Peter meant to say that "women were in a weaker position socially than men and their welfare depended upon their husbands' considerate treatment of them." She adds: "In terms of social status, women were inferior to men; but spiritually they are men's equals, and it is the spiritual reality that should guide the behavior of Christian husbands."[8] The idea was that a Christian husband was not to take his cues from the patriarchal and female-diminishing cultural viewpoint, but from the countercultural truths of his newfound Christian faith.

Finally, the Petrine text advises the Christian husband to show *time* toward his wife. Usually this Greek word *time* has been translated as "honor" or "respect." Of the two, respect is slightly preferable, since honor is more susceptible to misinterpretation (i.e., to signify a patronizing deference by opening doors, helping with heavy groceries, and lending an arm for support on icy streets). By contrast, respect is something to which one is *intrinsically* entitled, and I believe this is the sense intended in the text.

Spiritual consequences are tied to Peter's admonition. Husbands are to do these things so that their prayers may not be hindered. It is unclear how Christian husbands' treatment of their wives could possibly affect the effectiveness of their prayer life. Perhaps Peter means that we risk grieving the Holy Spirit when we relate to one another on the basis of obsolete gender protocols, for we are no longer completely in step with the Spirit. Those who persist in using the unfortunate phrase "the weaker vessel" in a pejorative way are committing precisely the fault that the apostle Peter was eager to eliminate from the social life of the church. He wanted Christian domestic relationships to reflect the same respectful mutuality that will exist in the kingdom to come, but which is not yet a fully restored reality on earth. This is what it means to be doing God's work today—bringing the future into the present, living ahead of the curve.

Men *and* Women Both Can Be Baptized

There are further signs of progress toward gospel ideals in the New Testament movement toward greater gender symmetry in religious and social affairs. Certainly there is a shift away from male privilege, as we saw in Old Testament society, to more bilateral and balanced expressions of gender rights and responsibilities in the New. The view of women as the property of males, and under their "priestly" or proprietary jurisdiction, is clearly in decline. Women are treated as the men's equal counterparts, and statements and prescriptions in the New Testament reflect this more recent validation of women by Christ and his empowering Spirit.

In matters of religious life, we see this in the new rite of initiation into the community of God's people. The Old Testament initiatory rite was male circumcision. This was the physical means by which a male child was publicly incorporated into the covenant people and their faith, and entitled to the privileges associated with being a Jew. No rite existed for female children. Women were considered part of the chosen people by reason of their association with Israelite men. They did not qualify directly or personally for this privilege, but indirectly and secondhand through the fathers and husbands to whom they were related. This arrangement was consistent with the subordinate status of women in the Old Testament era.

But things changed with the advent of the church as the new people of God. There is still an important place for a public right of initiation, but circumcision will no longer do as that rite. Instead, water baptism becomes the new rite of initiation. Its significance lies not only in its superiority as a symbol for the many new truths of redemption, but also in the fact that it is a rite in which both men *and women* now participate. Women now enter into the body of Christ as individuals in their own right, publicly professing their *own* faith, and having the reality of their own conversion etched on their souls in this edifying way. Christian women as well as men are able to participate in this powerful sign and seal of their personal identification with the death and resurrection of Christ. From the moment of beginning, then, Christian faith gives more recognition to female disciples than the traditions of Judaism allowed.

It would be wrong to assume that this gender-inclusive feature of the new initiation rite of baptism was merely coincidental. Right before Paul declares in Galatians 3:28 that in Christ there is neither male nor female, he notes that "all of you who were baptized into Christ have clothed yourselves with Christ" (v. 27). It is very likely that these two concepts—baptism and equality—are linked in Paul's mind. Because Galatians 3:28 was actually part of the liturgical language used in early Christian baptismal ceremonies, we must conclude that early Christians appreciated the egalitarian significance of this inclusive rite.

Priesthood of All Believers

The Levitical priests served as mediators between Israel and their God. The priests were important custodians of institutional religion, spiritual leaders, and authority figures for Judaism. Eventually they shared power with scribes and other experts in the Law, but they retained a key ministry role in the Old Testament religious order. Ordinary people could not approach God directly; those who wanted to connect with God had to go through a priest. It was obviously a great privilege to be able to minister on behalf of Yahweh. Those who aspired to this office of priest were obliged to meet rigorous qualifications—qualifications that excluded, among others, all women and disabled persons.

The New Testament displays a profound change in the concept of priesthood. In one sense it is eliminated; in another, it expands. Priesthood as practiced in the Old Testament became obsolete because, as the book of Hebrews explains, the entire sacrificial system was passé, and the role of priest was fulfilled in Jesus Christ, the perfect high priest. In this sense, priesthood was *eliminated*. On the other hand, the role of priest, in the sense of having direct access to God and authority to minister in his name, was now *widened* to include every Christian—men and women alike. *All* Christians now, regardless of gender or other restrictive criteria, qualified as members of the new "holy priesthood" (1 Peter 2:5, 9). Everyone who named the name of Christ was now a "priest." The sacrifices they now offered were no longer atoning ones, but sacrifices of gratitude, radical personal consecration, and good deeds in service to others (1 Peter 2:5; Rom. 12:1; Heb. 13:15–16). This new sense of Christian identity was known as "the priesthood of all believers." It was a doctrine particularly treasured by those who challenged oppression in church and state. The apparatus of religious middle-management, spiritual stratification, and hierarchical control collapses when every Christian receives God's grace directly and ministers to others in the name of Christ.

More Gender Symmetry

The Christian vision of egalitarianism is not restricted to "spiritual" matters. It is meant to affect social relationships as well, including that most intimate of human relationships, the marital bond. The dynamics of marriage, and the privileges and responsibilities of the two partners, are also presented in a reciprocal way in the New Testament. This is true of sexual intimacy (1 Cor. 7:2–5). One benefit of Christian marriage is that it provides a moral outlet for sexual energy and thus serves as a hedge against immorality. But the apostle Paul's explanation of this point is perfectly symmetrical: "Each man should have [sexual relations with] his own wife, and each woman [with] her own husband" (v. 2).

DIAGRAM 7.1. Gender Symmetry in Paul's Thought

---

1 CORINTHIANS 6–7

Dynamics of **Sexual Intimacy** (7:2–5)

Legal Rights in Marriage (7:10–13)

Spiritual Influence in the Home (7:14–16)

Future Honors and Responsibilities (6:22)

The pattern continues in the next verse, where Paul explains that "the husband should fulfill his marital duty to his wife, and likewise the wife to her husband" (v. 3). Not only that, but the wife is to yield authority over her body to her husband and the husband to yield authority over his body to his wife (v. 4). The Jewish male mind-set would have affirmed the first half of each of these statements of duty, but probably balked at the second half. The symmetrical quality of Paul's thinking continues in his concluding remark that a couple should temporarily abstain from sexual intimacy only by "mutual consent" (v. 5). In other words, the wife should have some say—an equal say, in fact—in deciding such matters.

Gender parallelism continues in Paul's discussion of the legal and public aspects of Christian marriage and, in particular, to the sensitive issues of separation and divorce (1 Cor. 7:10–11). In keeping with Jesus' strong opposition to divorce, Paul declares that a woman should not separate from her husband, and then immediately adds that a husband must not divorce his wife. There is no indication that a husband is more entitled to initiate a divorce than his wife or that the legitimate threshold for male dissatisfaction with a spouse should be lower than the threshold of the female. Instead, Paul teaches that neither a wife nor a husband should initiate the dissolution of their marriage. And it makes no difference whether one spouse is a believer and the other is not. The sanctity of marriage stands in spite of such spiritual inequality. The Christian husband must not divorce his unbelieving wife, and (here is the symmetry again) the Christian wife must not divorce her unbelieving husband.

This is because a Christian partner's influence in a marriage is not affected by his or her gender (1 Cor. 7:14–16). The unbelieving wife and children are "sanctified" by the Christian husband, just as the unbelieving husband and children are "sanctified" by the Christian wife. The spiritual power and influence of men is not any greater than that of women. A faithful wife may well be the instrument God uses to lead her husband to salvation, and a faithful husband may become the instrument God uses for the salvation of his wife. Contrary to some thinking today, the Christian husband is no more a "priest" for his spouse and family than his life partner is. In the New Testament age of grace, God uses men and women equally.

Gender symmetry is also evident in the church's vision of the future. One of the consolations of persecuted Christians was that they would some day be vindicated, just as Jesus had promised when he said that the poor in spirit would inherit the earth. Though they were suffering as victims of injustice, it was only for a time. Someday they would reign with Christ and judge the earth. The tables would be turned, and the victims would become the victors.

Reigning and judging are among the highest roles of leadership and authority in human society. Significantly, neither of these functions is restricted to male Christians. *Christians* will reign with Christ (2 Tim. 2:12). Christ's *servants* will reign forever and ever (Rev. 22:3–5), and the *saints* will judge the earth (1 Cor. 6:2). There is no hint that only male Christians will be asked to assume these roles. Presumably, female Christians will spend eternity doing more than serving tea. These functions will be performed by men and women alike in the *future* God has planned for us. Logically, then, we should try to align ourselves with this future and seek to make it, insofar as we are able, a reality in the here and now. As we say in the Lord's Prayer, "Your kingdom come, your will be done on earth as it is in heaven."

Apostolic Partnerships in Ministry

In conclusion, let us also consider the evidence of women function-
ing as leaders in the early church. The promptings of the Spirit produced more than just new doctrines. They altered the way Christians
lived and behaved in everyday life. It is not hard to see that the apostle Paul forged partnerships with women for the purpose of ministry
at various levels. In the epistles of the New Testament we have what
R. T. France has described as "the artless disclosure of what in fact was
going on."[9] In Philippi, the embarrassing rift between Euodia and
Syntyche, two women whom Paul nevertheless describes as his
coworkers, was high profile enough to unsettle church fellowship.[10]
In addition, Paul had a habit of acknowledging Christian couples *as
couples* in his epistles, a literary practice that implicitly acknowledges
the importance of both marriage partners to the work of the early
church. Women were no longer invisible in the new community that
was coming into being.

One of the most intriguing associates of the apostles was the
married-couple team of Priscilla and Aquila. These were evidently
prominent companions of the apostle Paul, Jewish friends who traveled with him to various places and worked alongside him in his tent-
making. One of their greatest successes in discipleship was to earn the
confidence of the eloquent Apollos, an up-and-coming Christian leader
from a strong Jewish background, and then draw him aside and
instruct him in the things of the Lord (Acts 18:24–26). It was one of
the most effective instances in the entire Bible of properly teaching a
man. Some have assumed that Priscilla figures in the New Testament
literature because she was willing to operate meekly under the
umbrella of her husband's authority. What is most intriguing, and effectively undermines such speculation, is that in most references to the
pair—toward whom Paul felt a deep affection and the highest regard—
the name of Priscilla is listed first (e.g., Acts 18:18). The most plausible explanation for this is that Priscilla was the more capable, or at
least the more forceful, personality of the two.

Lydia, a Greek businesswoman from Thyatira, was the first European convert to Christianity. A long way from home, she successfully

practiced a business for which her hometown was famous. Lydia was someone able to make her own way in the world. Immediately she invited Paul and his entourage into her home. "If you consider me a believer in the Lord," she urged, "come and stay at my house" (Acts 16:15). Evidently she extended this invitation unilaterally. From all appearances, she functioned as head of her household and lived a life of freedom and independence. Lydia proved instrumental in the apostle Paul gaining a toehold in this vast new mission field (v. 40).

Just as Jesus and his band of disciples had been sustained through the support of certain women of financial means (Mark 15:41), the apostle Paul and his associates were housed and supported by other women of comparable status. Not a few of the early house churches assembled and found sanctuary in the homes of wealthy women. In addition to Lydia, the list includes Mary the mother of John Mark (Acts 12:12), Chloe (1 Cor. 1:11), and Nympha (Col. 4:15). Though we should not underestimate their Spirit-filled graciousness, it seems improbable that such women of independence and influence would readily submit to demeaning estimations of their abilities and worth, or to harsh male demands for their complete silence and subservience in the church. To the contrary, one of the things that drew such women to early Christianity, and away from the pagan religious competition, was its empowering egalitarian ethos.

Women's names are frequently listed, and prominently, in the apostle Paul's correspondence. Take the extensive list of names at the conclusion of his epistle to the Romans, for example; a remarkable number of them (ten of twenty-seven, by one count) are female. And many of these women occupied positions of leadership in the various churches. At least one, Phoebe, is described as a deacon of the church in Corinth's port city of Cenchrea, and very possibly a patron or benefactor of that church (Rom. 16:1–2). The office of deacon had been an important one from the church's beginnings (Phil. 1:1), and Phoebe held it. For a long time Bible translators have quietly downgraded her role to that of "deaconess," or "servant," thereby making Paul's description of her more consistent with gender hierarchy in the church. But the truth is, there is nothing in the text itself to warrant such downscaling of her role.

A similar translation deception has recently come to light over Junia, who is described in Romans 16:7 as "outstanding among the apostles." For many years her name has been translated as Junias (the male name corresponding to Junia), even though there was actually less reliable manuscript support for this option. Junias was preferred, or so it appears, partly because the translators *assumed* that a woman would never have been "outstanding among the apostles." Paul explains that Andronicus and Junia were in Christ before he was, and it is possible that they were eyewitnesses to the resurrection. This might explain Paul's description of them as among the apostles—that is, using "apostles" in a still-privileged but broader sense than the Twelve. In any event, it is difficult to envision the woman Paul acknowledged here as one who silently supported her husband while contenting herself with hospitality and children's ministries.

The debate over these names and terms will no doubt persist for some time to come. Yet the language Paul uses in his references to various women, addressing them as dear and respected friends, sisters, mothers, hard-working colaborers, makes it seem most likely that the innovative early church had already moved well beyond strict adherence to the tired, old rules of patriarchy. They had caught the wave of the Spirit and were having the time of their lives.

chapter summary

The early church, true to its mission as the body of Christ, extended the trajectory of Christ's initiatives to liberate women. Pentecost was an enormous stimulus to gender equality. The apostle Paul taught that women and men were one in Christ, and Peter viewed the social disadvantages of women as a lingering problem, not God's will for the future. In matters ranging from baptism to marital relations, the church was moving toward greater gender symmetry. Women were prominent, and the apostles forged telling partnerships in ministry with male and female colleagues alike. There was indeed substantial progress toward gospel ideals, and every reason for optimism that the movement thus begun would continue in a progressive direction.

This statement based on what?

Questions for Individual or Group Reflection

1. How did Pentecost stimulate gender equality in the early church?

2. What did Paul mean when he declared that there is no longer male and female, for we are all one in Christ (Gal. 3:28)? Was he referring to more than our equal access to justification? Defend your interpretation.

3. Explain the real meaning of the familiar description of woman as "the weaker vessel" (1 Peter 3:7 KJV). How might this understanding of the phrase affect the way Christians treat women?

4. What do you find significant in the New Testament references to Priscilla?

5. Can you think of an example of gender symmetry in the New Testament? How does this compare to practices in the earlier age of patriarchy?

chapter 8

Old Habits Die Hard

the persistence of patriarchy

Luti got a first taste of her life's work during the summer of 1948 in rural Canada, where there were no men available to pastor, preach, or run camps. So she and a female friend did it all, traveling the gravel roads up around Lake Superior on their bicycles. From there it was on to decades of mission work in Belgian Congo, where she survived the turbulence of Congolese independence and the Lumumba uprisings. Years later, she handed over her duties to Zairians she had trained, and volunteered for a new assignment amid the killing fields of Cambodia.

During the final days of Phnom Penh, with Khymer Rouge rockets landing all around, she consoled despondent people and preached the gospel with authority. She led a group of eager Buddhist monks, who gathered in her apartment, through the gospel of John, and saw many of them converted. Afterward, she followed Cambodian survivors to refugee camps in Thailand. Retirement loomed, but instead she moved to southern France and continued evangelizing there, often door-to-door, for years. Recently she planned to participate in a bold prayer walk through the Middle East and was disappointed when it was canceled for security reasons. Her motto has been "to throw her life with reckless abandon into the face of human need." For the record, she's more wild at heart than most men I know.

Luti now has white hair, and dutifully dons ethnic dress and carries a national flag (she has, of course, several to pick from) at her denomination's colorful annual mission rallies. But for the most part she has learned to remain silent. She was not ordained. Her opinions are seldom solicited. She has not been a church elder or board member, and she is not usually invited to preach. Such weighty public responsibilities go to younger people—younger *men*, actually—who are a lot thinner in talent, life experience, and spiritual authority. But Luti is a woman, so, intrepid saint notwithstanding, she must be in submission.

It's a waste of refined insight and spiritual wisdom, isn't it? Of course it is! Sometimes, traveling alone on missionary deputation, she would be asked, by default, to "share" in a Sunday morning church service. She learned always to begin with a disclaimer that "the men have asked me to speak today." Many would find this demeaning, but she managed with uncommon grace. But *why* do churches behave like this? Ask their leaders. They'll probably answer by quoting things they've read in the New Testament. That's what we're going to do now. As we do, keep in mind that viewing isolated texts in light of the larger movement of Scripture is the surest way of interpreting them correctly.

As noted in the previous chapter, the early church made substantial progress toward the gender ideals Jesus introduced. It rode that wave and willingly extended the trajectory of the Spirit. But there was another bracing dimension to the situation back then. The early Christians lived in a man's world. Patriarchal attitudes prevailed where the gospel took root and persisted in the early Christian community itself. It was a less-than-perfect human fellowship. Ex-pagans and converted Jews, believers were learning as they went along what it meant to be Christians. They did not all at once begin to perfectly imitate the Christ they had come to love. Not all the default settings of their psyches were instantaneously switched over to reflect the full implications of the gospel they now embraced.

The inspired text of the New Testament is salted with vestiges of patriarchy. They consist of little things, like the way the gospel writers estimated crowd sizes. In the miracle of the five loaves and two fishes, for example, Matthew reported that "the number of those who ate was about five thousand *men*, besides women and children" (Matt. 14:21, my emphasis). Obviously the number of men was the significant demographic for Matthew, and the women and children were added the way a baseball trade might be announced nowadays, with some minor leaguers "to be named later" thrown in.

At the other end of the New Testament, John described in his Revelation an elite group of 144,000 believers who stand in special relationship to the Lamb. Their moral purity is depicted in these terms: "These are those who did not defile themselves with women" (Rev. 14:4). Female Christians may feel understandably slighted by their exclusion from the ranks of the 144,000, and perhaps also by the suggestion that sexual contact with women is defiling. The New Testament displays patriarchal residue that female readers are obliged to see *through* in order to grasp and own its liberating message.

Paul as Pragmatist in the Real World

Any discussion of gender in the New Testament must deal with statements of the apostle Paul—a visionary who grasped the revolutionary implications of faith in the resurrected Christ. He was also a pragmatic entrepreneur who understood what it took to make it in the real world. He was prepared to stand up and be counted when he believed that a principle was at stake. He challenged the apostle Peter "to his face" when he judged that Peter had strayed from the gospel truth of freedom from the law (Gal. 2:11). However, Paul was also willing to make calculated concessions for the sake of greater goals. Before taking Timothy on a missions trip, Paul had him circumcised "because of the Jews" (Acts 16:3). Later, to reassure believers in Jerusalem who were uneasy about his message to Gentiles, he underwent a Jewish purification rite and paid the expenses for four other Christian Jews to do the same (Acts 21:20–26). He could, in his own phrase, "become all things to all people" (1 Cor. 9:22 TNIV).

So part of Paul's persona was that of a pragmatist—still principled, but one who always kept his ultimate goals in mind. His *chief* aim was to see the good news of the resurrected Christ proclaimed in a clear, compelling way. This meant that a credible image for the new faith had to be established and maintained. Everything had to be done in such a way that offense was minimal, and prejudices and false rumors were nipped in the bud.

Paul stressed the need to "walk worthy" (Col. 1:10 KJV) of the gospel, to conduct oneself in ways that commended Christ. As much as possible, Christians needed to earn reputations as good citizens who paid their taxes, submitted to civil authorities, and minded their own business. Their goal was not to precipitate an immediate overturn of the existing social order. Rather, they wanted to live peaceful lives in all godliness so that they could devote their energy to personal evangelism and church building.

In the movie *Witness* (1985), directed by gifted Australian Peter Weir, Harrison Ford plays the part of John Book, a slick city cop who has to lay low for a while in an Amish community in Lancaster County, Pennsylvania. To fit into that peculiar society and avoid detection, Book starts riding around in a plain horse and buggy. He adopts the boots, suspenders, work shirt, and big black hat that are standard issue for Amish men. He even begins to grow a patriarchal beard. The Amish people have historical and religious reasons for dressing like this. Book identifies with neither, but he goes along with the dress code for pragmatic reasons. The apostle Paul behaved similarly when it came to first-century social protocols.

Now the early Christians lived in a highly stratified society, one which included Roman citizens and non-citizens, patriarchs and their households, masters and slaves, and (from a Jewish perspective, at least) chosen Jews and less-favored Gentiles. Likewise men and women were viewed through the lens of an ideology of male superiority and female inferiority, and gender roles were assigned accordingly. Men were the leaders (the heads, if you will), and women (at least *good* women) were submissive and obedient—first to their fathers, and then, following marriage, to their husbands.

Paul's usual advice to believers was to find meaning in life through acceptance of these realities rather than by raging against them. He was very explicit about accepting one's lot in life, whether that lot involved slavery, marriage, or a particular cultural heritage. "Each of you," he instructed, "should live as a believer in whatever situation the Lord has assigned to you, just as God has called you" (1 Cor. 7:17 TNIV).

Living with Slavery and Gender Privilege

Paul challenged the Jewish assumption of religious superiority with all his might. He was convinced that the gospel could never be reconciled to a system of ethnic preference and privilege. To capitulate to such a violation of gospel freedom would be to embrace another gospel altogether. The Jew-Gentile distinction, precious to Jews and odious to Gentiles, could not be tolerated. Ethnic hierarchy had to be dismantled so that salvation in Christ could be made equally available to all, and the church could develop in the unity of the Spirit without any levels within its fellowship. Nothing less would do.

However, Paul didn't seem to view the dismantling of the hierarchical systems of slavery and gender privilege with the same priority or urgency. To be sure, slaves and masters, women and men, were both welcomed into the new community of faith. Yet women and slaves were not strongly encouraged to seek the social emancipation implicit in their spiritual liberation in Christ. For practical reasons, the old social distinctions of sexism and slavery still needed to be observed. Paul was prudently concerned for the reputation and image of the new faith community. The message of the cross was scandalous enough without the scandal being unnecessarily compounded.

In this frame of mind Paul considered the power-differentiated relationships between fathers and children, masters and slaves, and husbands and wives (Col. 3:17–4:1; Eph. 5:22–6:9). He explained to the respective parties in each of these relationships how they should now view their responsibilities. Those who temporarily enjoyed the upper hand (fathers, masters, and husbands) were to lead in the self-giving and gentle way that Christ modeled. Those who stood on the lower rungs of the social ladder (that is, children, slaves, and wives) were to do more than fulfill socially prescribed obligations to their earthly parent, human master, or marriage partner. In their acts of submission they were to see themselves serving *Christ*, who was infinitely worthy of their service. Rather than becoming preoccupied with escape from their disadvantaged social roles, slaves and women were to focus on fulfilling the expectations imposed on them by the existing social order and do so in a way that would earn the approval of unbelievers.

This does not mean that the apostle personally endorsed these hierarchical social institutions. It simply means that under Paul's direction the early church was to soften the harsher edges and more acute outrages associated with these systems, rather than to rise up in revolution against them. Christians could look ahead to times more favorable to radical social transformation. But for the immediate future, they were to quietly advance the gospel, knowing that it carried hidden within itself, like the Trojan horse, a power to eventually change everything.

Paul's strategy was socially conservative. Understandably, questions arise about his willingness to tolerate the oppressive first-century institutions of slavery and sexism. Speculation will continue over whether missionary pragmatism is sufficient explanation for the relative insensitivity to the plights of first-century slaves and women that Paul appears to display. What exactly was going on in his mind? We cannot be entirely sure. It is sufficient to remember that the Spirit of God can, if necessary, breathe out inspired and truthful Scripture through the instrumentality of writers who still only "know in part" (1 Cor. 13:12).

Required Head-Coverings

Of particular interest to us are some gender-related texts that tell us what Paul expected of first-century Christians. After clarifying his expectations, we will examine the *arguments* he offered in support of his instructions. In many ways his supporting arguments have become more significant than his practical instructions themselves. These arguments warrant our most careful consideration, since they have been interpreted in ways that have profoundly affected the place of women in Christianity.

We begin with what Paul considered appropriate dress during times of corporate worship. He had no problem with women praying and prophesying out loud, or otherwise fully participating, alongside men in these services. The apostle insisted in 1 Corinthians 11:2–16 that women should wear culturally appropriate head-coverings (probably shawls, possibly veils) when they participated in such services. The best explanation for Paul's insistence on female head-coverings is that they symbolized submission to male authority and conformed to cultural standards of modesty and propriety.

A head-covering, then, was a culturally appropriate sign that a vocal, actively participating Christian woman still acknowledged the higher authority of men (and was a modest person as well). Without such an outward symbol of her heart attitude, her public prayers, prophesying, and other contributions to public worship might have been viewed as acts of defiance of the widely assumed concept of male headship. Paul described the head-covering as an *exousia*, which means "authority" or "sign of authority." Whenever she wore such a thing, a Christian woman's credentials were considered in place, and she was thereby fully *authorized* to contribute to communal worship.

Paul's instruction was a judicious accommodation to prevailing sensibilities. This interpretation is strengthened by the fact that he had just finished saying: "Do not cause anyone to stumble, whether Jews, Greeks or the church of God—even as I try to please everybody in every way" (1 Cor. 10:32–33). What remains to be determined, of course, is whether Paul himself "bought into" the concept of male headship as a foundational truth for all time. Reasons will be offered in a moment to support the conclusion that probably he did not.

Orderly Worship

A wonderful new spirit of female liberation was present in the church at Corinth. Gone were barriers to women being significant partners in ministry. Gone were the synagogue screens dividing men from women, along with the prohibitions of women praying and prophesying in the worshiping congregations. But recently liberated Christian women did not always have the knowledge or maturity to handle their newfound freedoms well. The Jewish and Greco-Roman patriarchal systems, which had for so long stifled women's personal growth, were to blame for this, not women themselves. A revolution was indeed underway, and like all revolutions it got a bit messy at times. Occasionally situations arose in which the behavior of recently liberated Christian women ran to immature excess, to the discrediting of the church, and the embarrassment of Paul himself.

Paul addressed this situation in 1 Corinthians 14:33–40. Early Christian worship services were patterned after those of the synagogues. If these were anything like Orthodox Jewish services today, they were casual and conversational in style. A lot was going on in a synagogue while the Torah was being read. Paul wanted Christian worship to be edifying, thoughtful, and thought-provoking. Christians were to exercise gifts responsibly and prioritize the most helpful ones. Worship services were to be peaceful and characterized by restraint. Things had to be done in "a fitting and orderly way" (v. 40), and Christians needed to think about how their conduct might appear to seekers (14:23–25).

It appears that some women were speaking out confrontationally in worship services, and some (perhaps the same ones) were disrupting the meetings by asking strings of questions and chattering among themselves about matters they found confusing. Paul's response was that such women needed to remain silent and should not be allowed to speak in this way. Instead, they were to assume an attitude of submission toward the speakers and worship leaders, and ask any questions they might have of their husbands later at home.

It makes no sense to infer from this that Christian women should be mute in church services. How unlikely that Paul would contradict the documented practice of female participation in worship services, or place valued coworkers like Phoebe and Priscilla under a gag order! Isn't it far more reasonable to interpret Paul's remarks in the same sense as a strict professor might say: "I do not permit talking in my classes." Such a professor might actually welcome good discussions and enjoy being challenged from time to time, but everyone knows exactly what she means when she says this (i.e., things must not get out of hand). Just so, when Paul said that women (and surely he meant a particular subgroup of noisy and distracting women) were not allowed to speak, he meant that such women were not to be talking while the worship service was going on. They were to stop distracting others and to abstain from impertinent comments, grandstanding, and domineering speech of any kind at all. His underlying reason was that "God is not a God of disorder but of peace" (14:33).

Paul concluded: "It is disgraceful for a woman to speak in the church" (v. 35). He meant that it was disgraceful for a woman to speak *like that* in the church. The truth is, it would be disgraceful for *anyone*, man *or* woman, to speak like that in the church, but it so happened that the culprits in this instance (because of the social and educational disadvantages they had known in their formative years) were chiefly women.

Resisting a Hostile Takeover Bid

Paul touched on gender again in his response to a hostile, antimale bid to take control of the Christian assembly in Ephesus. Evidently a faction there had been influenced by a heretical teaching, possibly from the Artemis (Diana) cult so central to the culture and economy of that city.[1] Plausibly the heresy involved the notion that women were superior to men in spiritual insight (and ought therefore to be their teachers), and that domestic responsibilities were beneath their dignity. In an inversion of patriarchy, this cult actually privileged women over men, and its otherworldly creed sneered at both marriage and childbearing.[2]

The apostle considered such thinking twisted. Women with such inflated opinions of themselves needed to recover a humbler, more biblical self-understanding. And they needed to return to the God-ordained institution of marriage and to be willing to help raise families. They were encouraged to continue learning (and such encouragement put Christianity on the progressive edge of first-century society), but they were to do so in a submissive spirit that had been conspicuously lacking to that point. In this context Paul declared that "woman should learn in quietness and full submission" (1 Tim. 2:11). To be quiet in this instance meant not to be disruptive. To be in full submission meant not to be impudent. It did not mean that women were reduced to sign language and passing notes.

Paul continued: "I do not permit a woman to teach (*didaskein*) or to have authority over (*authentein*) a man" (v. 12). This statement has been the eye of the storm in Christian discussions of gender roles ever since. The key to unlocking its enigma lies in the original words themselves. The Greek term for "have authority" (*authentein*) occurs in the

New Testament only here, but from other surviving literature of this period we know that it was a particularly strong word suggesting domination, inappropriate control, or lording it over someone.[3]

Likewise, the word meaning "to teach" (*didaskein*) has a range of possible meanings that extends from conveying information to telling someone what to do.[4] Given the grammatical parallel between *authentein* and *didaskein* in Paul's statement, we should also take *didaskein* in its more assertive and confrontational sense. In effect, Paul was saying that he did not permit a woman to *lecture* or be *domineering* toward a man. Everything is in the nuance. Rather than banning women from instructional and leadership roles *per se*, he was denouncing *pushiness*, because it undermined the ultimate goal of harmony and mutuality.

The Tone of Paul's Remarks

Reviewing Paul's responses to these three practical issues—head-coverings, orderly worship, and a hostile church takeover bid—reveals nothing sexist about the *positions* he took. Each of his proposals was measured and reasonable. Regarding mandatory female head-coverings, the strongest criticism that can be leveled against him is that he was not sensitive enough to the plight of oppressed first-century Christian women, and the extent of the unequal burden he was calling them to continue bearing for the sake of the gospel's reputation among outsiders.

In his instructions for reestablishing decorum in Corinthian worship, the only thing on which Paul might possibly be criticized is *how* he expressed himself. He exhibits, admittedly, a severity in his manner of expression. Paul's statement comes across as a sweeping generalization, without any qualifying phrases or caveats to acknowledge the many spiritually mature women who were making valued contributions, verbal and otherwise, to the worship and work of the church. "Women should remain silent" (1 Cor. 14:34), he said—not *some* women, or *those* women, or the *troublesome* ones—but just *women*. The Paul who wrote Galatians did not believe that women in general were the problem. Nevertheless, it would have been nice if he had made this clearer here.

In retrospect, Paul's pastoral directives seem reasonable enough. Few Christians today, once they understand what was actually going on, and what Paul was really saying, should have major problems with his proposals. However, Paul's arguments in support of his practical recommendations have been more controversial, and, unfortunately, more frequently misunderstood. They have shaped historic Christian understandings of gender more than his instructions themselves. The most important of these are the concept of male headship and his inferences from the Genesis stories of creation and the fall.

A Fresh Look at Male Headship

Have you ever considered what a difference the translation of a single word in the New Testament can make? Consider this example. In his letter to the Ephesians, Paul described the husband as the *kephale* of the wife (Eph. 5:23). In his communication with the Corinthians, Paul portrayed the man as the *kephale* of the woman (1 Cor. 11:3). In this latter case, the term extends beyond marriage to all gender relations. Traditionally, this word has been translated into English as "head," and consequently been understood to indicate leadership and authority. Today discussion circulates around whether "head" is a translator's best choice, since the range of meanings of the English word "head" does not match exactly that of the Greek word *kephale*.

Indeed, the English word "head" has strong connotations of authority, perhaps stronger ones than *kephale* conveyed. Conversely, the cognate idea of "source," though still present in the English word "head" (for example, the headwaters of a river), is probably not conveyed as forcefully as it was through *kephale* to a first-century Greek audience. This said, however, we can't cut out all connotations of preeminence, authority, and leadership from *kephale*. The term can carry both the sense of preeminent authority *and* the sense of providing nourishment and life. As such, it has a richer, thicker meaning than is conveyed by the English word "head." Yet it still depicts the male standing in a hierarchical relationship of authority to the woman, with a natural converse of submission on the woman's part. The concept of authority is probably always in the background.[5]

The more important question is the status of this imagery of *kephale*. Does it represent God's timeless design for the man's relationship to the woman, or is it instead an apt symbol of the estimate of a man's place, compared to a woman's, in first-century Greek society? Is the Scripture accommodating itself at this point to an entrenched social convention, or laying down a normative understanding for the church for all time?

In light of the trajectory of the Spirit, we are convinced that Paul is not teaching male headship as normative for believers. Instead, he accepts it as a working premise for what he is about to say to his Christian readers. He is not advising Christians that they should think of the man as the head of the woman, despite unbelievers failing to understand this revealed truth. Rather, he is acknowledging that male headship is a cultural "given." "Since everyone already shares this assumption of male headship," Paul seems to be saying, "let's consider how we can 'baptize' it, and, to the extent possible here in the first century, bring it into line with the transforming genius of our faith in Jesus Christ."

Two Arguments from Genesis

In some evangelical circles there is a great deal of talk about how the apostle Paul based his counsel on "normative truths" drawn from the biblical stories of creation and the fall. Some evangelicals have argued that Paul's instructions cannot be restricted to a particular historical context, since they are actually grounded in the creation order itself— in transcultural and unchanging theological principles. Two such Pauline arguments presuppose that Adam and Eve embody, respectively, the essence of maleness and femaleness. Both arguments assume that males inherit Adam's tendencies and privileges, and women inherit Eve's predisposition and liabilities.

In the first argument, Paul declared pointedly that "Adam was formed first, then Eve" (1 Tim. 2:13). His argument, simply put, was that since Adam came first in the order of creation, men are in some ways superior to, and should be above, women. This is the old notion of primogeniture (that is, that the firstborn should always be privileged). Elsewhere Paul elaborates on this basic view of things: "For man did not come from woman, but woman *from* man; neither was man created for woman, but woman *for* man" (1 Cor. 11:8–9, my emphasis). Women should be subordinate to men because Eve owed her existence to Adam, and also because she was created *for* him, that is, to provide for his needs by serving and assisting him. Eve's derivation from Adam's side gave him a priority status above her, and her reason for existence was ultimately to serve his needs. Ultimately women depend upon men for their existence, and exist for men's purposes.

The other argument draws on the story of the fall, and it goes like this: While Adam was first in the order of creation, Eve proved herself in the early going to be the more gullible of the two. Consequently she (and, of course, all women after her) is in some way permanently inferior to the man. Again Paul states the matter bluntly: "Adam was not the one deceived; it was the woman who was deceived and became a sinner" (1 Tim. 2:14).

What a shocking statement! Superiority has already been attributed to the male on the basis of Adam's chronological primacy. Inferiority is now conferred on women on the basis of Eve's deception and decision to sin. Thus Eve, the archetypal woman, is second in the order of creation but first in the order of sinning. The implication is clear: the woman is morally inferior, or at least more gullible—liabilities that should disqualify her from strategic roles of influence, including teaching and leadership.

These statements suggest that because they were second in creation order, but first in sinful deception, women are less. Note that this is *more* than a claim to functional subordination; women are by *nature* inferior to, and less than, men. Female inferiority is of essence and not just function. Just laying out these gender allegations in plain speech exposes how alien they really are to the spirit of the New Testament gospel.

Echoes of "Rabbi Talk"

Did Paul really mean that the Genesis stories of human creation and the fall teach divinely sanctioned and permanent principles of gender hierarchy? The answer must be a resounding No! Such spins on the ancient accounts are actually *rabbi talk*. We do not find any of the Old

Testament writers themselves drawing such inferences from the Genesis stories. This is significant. It means that this way of thinking was not biblical—it came in later history. Paul's remarks echo views developed later, between the Testaments—prejudices nurtured in the rabbinic circles in which Paul once moved and excelled. "Within the *synagogue*, which provided a model for early church life and structure, male dominance was traditionally certified by a reading of the chronological sequence of Genesis 2 in terms of male priority." Moreover, from the account of the fall the *rabbinic* tradition concluded that "women were by nature more vulnerable to deception than men."[6] These ideas represent the classic post-exilic Jewish patriarchal spin on the Genesis narrative, not the intent of the Old Testament writers themselves.

Moreover, a fair-minded reader has to acknowledge an *intrinsic weakness* to these rabbinic-style arguments. As John Calvin recognized 450 years ago, the argument for Adam's primacy has logical problems. According to such a test, suggested Calvin, John the Baptist would be superior to his younger cousin Jesus,[7] and the same could be said concerning the creation account of all the vegetables and creeping things that predated the origins of Adam. If primogeniture was the key principle in the creation story, humans are the lowest of the low.

The story of Eve's creation from Adam's side was actually intended to underscore her equality to him—bone of his bone, and flesh of his flesh (Gen. 2:23). Such rabbis missed the theological point. Moreover, Eve was created as a partner corresponding to Adam, as his perfect equal and not as his Girl Friday. And as for the rabbis' scapegoating of the woman for human sin, it is hard to figure out from the Genesis account itself how the sin of the woman was *in any way* more culpable than the man's.

A Case Study to Help Us Interpret Paul

First Corinthians 11:3–16 provides a very helpful case study for determining how we ought to interpret Paul's assertion of male headship and his rabbinic-style arguments from Genesis. The passage contains instances of both, and I invite you to take the time to read it carefully (like a good Berean) before proceeding.

Did you notice the weakness of the other arguments with which the headship and primogeniture ones are bundled together here? In other words, the plausibility of these positions is *weakened by association*. See how Paul argues that the man is the image and glory of God, while the woman is the glory of man (v. 7). He comes within a whisker of contradicting the foundational Christian truth that both women and men image God equally. But even as it stands, it exudes the spirit of those rabbis who alleged that woman's claim to God's image was secondary to, and derivative from, man's.

DIAGRAM 8.1. The Case for Female Head-Coverings

Paul's Arguments for Head-Coverings from 1 Corinthians 11:3–16

Male **Headship** (v. 3)

Levels of **Glory** (v. 7)

Order of **Creation** (vv. 8–9)

Because of the **Angels** (v. 10)

What **Nature** Teaches (vv. 14–15)

Appeal to **Convention** (v. 16)

Paul also suggests that even nature teaches us that men should wear short hair and women long hair (vv. 14–15). Does it really? Are we really prepared to say that it is *against nature* for Native American men to grow their hair long in the traditional way, or that the shorter contemporary hairstyles of women in America are sinful? But taken at face value, this is what the apostle appears to be saying. We must conclude that the intuitive knowledge of nature's ways, to which Paul makes his appeal, was probably more culturally conditioned than his statement acknowledges.

Finally, the casual way in which the apostle presented these arguments (and others, like the passing one about the angels) and bundled them all up together, suggests that they may not reflect his own deepest personal convictions. Note how, in the end, he throws his hands up in what appears to be a rather weak appeal to convention: "If any-one wants to be contentious about this, we have no other practice—nor do the churches of God" (v. 16). In other words, this is the way we have always done things. John Calvin, one of history's most devout students of Scripture, recognized that Paul was "often in the habit" of using arguments that do not deserve to be treated as normative theo-logical principles.[8] This chapter in 1 Corinthians is probably a good example of what Calvin was driving at.

The Art of Persuasion

Why would Paul talk about male headship, or draw these inferences from the stories of creation and the fall, unless he personally believed them to be so? The answer is that the apostle was appealing to the assumptions, and even prejudices, of his audience, for the purpose of persuading them about something on *their own terms*. Personally, Paul did not completely buy *kephale*, or these Jewish arguments from creation and the fall, but he was willing to lay them out whenever he calculated that they might carry weight with audiences who still thought along these lines. He argued this way to make his directive more acceptable to socially conservative groups within the New Testament churches.

I am not just pulling this out of a hat. This is not the only instance of the apostle Paul using this rhetorical technique. For example, in the course of making his best case for the certainty of a future bodily res-urrection, Paul reasoned: "Now if there is no resurrection, what will those do who are baptized for the dead? If the dead are not raised at all, why are people baptized for them?" (1 Cor. 15:29). It is highly doubtful that this baptismal practice was one that Paul himself endorsed, yet he is quick to reference it to make his real point more convincing *to his audience*.[9]

And here's another example. Paul used this same argumentative tactic in Ephesians 4:8, where he quotes Psalm 68:18 to the effect that "when he [Christ] ascended on high, he led captives in his train and *gave* gifts to men." This reading echoed a popular Jewish liturgical spin on the text at the time. But Paul, as a rabbinic scholar, would certainly have known that the actual Hebrew text of Psalm 68, then as now, says that the Lord *received* gifts (that is, tribute) from men. Tongue in cheek, then, Paul willingly exploits what was usefully at hand to make an important point about Christ as the true source of the gifts of the Spirit.[10] It is very doubtful that the apostle ever intended that these arguments, or, more accurately, these *rhetorical devices*, should be taken as enduring principles and permanent norms for the church.

The Clincher

The most compelling evidence against treating either Paul's concept of male headship, or his arguments from human creation and the fall, as normative, is this: Paul eventually acknowledges that the arguments we have been reviewing in 1 Corinthians 11 are actually inconsistent with his gospel. "In the Lord," he admits, there is to be gender interdependence rather than hierarchy. Men depend on women for their existence just as much as women depend on men for theirs (1 Cor. 11:11–12). You cannot say that the woman exists for the man any more than the man exists for her. In the Lord—that is, from the perspective of truth as it is in Jesus—none of this hierarchy stuff holds water anymore. In the Lord this whole rabbinic spin is suspect. And so we must ask, rhetorically: For what conceivable reason would any Christian today want to continue living according to obsolete hierarchical notions instead of living "in the Lord"?

We should treat these so-called normative creational principles for what they really were—pragmatic arguments laid out in order to persuade. Paul could still play the part of a rabbi and use the old rabbinic style to make some points. He could appear to be defending his position from Scripture, when in fact he was simply illustrating his point by a homiletic flourish or two. Tongue in cheek, Paul willingly exploited what was usefully at hand to make his case. By doing so, he discredited neither himself nor his writings. Authoritative Scripture includes a broad variety of human conversation styles.

Adamic Headship

One last bit of patriarchal thinking in the New Testament needs an explanation. One of the apostle Paul's many brilliant theological flourishes came when he compared Adam with Jesus Christ. Paul developed this analogy between the first Adam of Genesis and Jesus Christ (the second Adam) in his treatments of justification (Rom. 5) and the resurrection (1 Cor. 15). Paul used the term "Adam" to designate the original man Adam as distinct from his wife, Eve. The analogy is set up, as one writer has put it, on the assumption that both Adam and Christ "acted representatively so that what each did has incalculable consequences for those he heads."[11]

Initially, Paul's analogy between the two Adams (and their respective "Adam families") appears problematic for our thesis, as it privileges Adam (the male) over Eve (the female) as the official head of the human race. The analogy rests on the assumption that only Adam acted and spoke for all humanity. Though according to Genesis Eve sinned first, Adam's sin is here treated as of greater significance: "Sin entered the world through one man" (Rom. 5:12). The same prioritizing of Adam is implicit in Paul's suggestion that "in Adam all die" (1 Cor. 15:22). How ironic that we should have to insist that Eve's sin was just as consequential as Adam's. But the difficulty is that the assumption of male priority, upon which this analogy is built, falls below the biblical vision of restored gender mutuality.

The apostle Paul, true to form, was willing to adapt to a prevailing mind-set in order to proclaim the significance of Christ in terms that his hearers could understand. The Jews of this era held Eve (and thus all women) responsible for allowing sin to enter the world. But while the woman was *instrumentally* responsible for sin, it was ultimately Adam's sin, not hers (because Adam was the official leader), that was decisive for humanity. The idea was that Adam was the official head of the human race, and original sin started with him.

Paul himself had likely already moved beyond this assumption of male priority. But if he exploded this notion right here, his entire two-Adam analogy would break down. Keep in mind that the formal headship of Adam does not need to be an actual fact any more than, say, Hamlet must be real (as opposed to a Shakespearean creation) before any literary analogies to the brooding Danish prince can be valid. Someone as "depressed as Hamlet" can still be genuinely depressed.

With respect to Paul's two-Adam analogy, the patriarchal assumption implicit in it can likewise be discarded while the inspired truth remains intact that in Christ the human race has the potential for a new beginning and hope of immortality.

It should probably not surprise us that the apostle was relatively indifferent toward the full social liberation of women, or establishing egalitarian relationships, since he no longer considered the existing world all that important. The best way to make our peace with Paul on these matters is to remember that he expected that Christ would return very soon, and that the time left was indeed short (1 Cor. 7:29). It was not revealed to Paul that history would continue on for another two thousand years. Nor did he know that the *ad hoc* instructions he gave to faithful clusters of believers scattered around the Mediterranean would achieve the stature of sacred Scripture for centuries to come. Had he known all this, he might very well have developed with more careful intentionality the themes of gender equality, freedom, and mutuality which were already implicit in his gospel. As the apostle Peter acknowledged, some things in Paul's writings are harder to understand than others (2 Peter 3:16), but they are still God-breathed, and therefore, *when properly interpreted*, are an infallible guide for Christian faith and practice.

chapter summary

The New Testament contains clear evidence of the gospel ideals of gender equality, freedom, and mutuality. On the other hand, it also reflects apostolic accommodations to first-century social norms, along with instances of rabbinic-style argumentation in support of them. All this Scripture is useful for teaching, rebuking, correcting, and training in righteousness (2 Tim. 3:16), but not all of it has proven equally easy to interpret. This is the biblical legacy that the post-apostolic church inherited almost two thousand years ago. And thus the stage was set for the church's long journey back to the garden of Eden.

Questions for Individual or Group Reflection

1. Do you think the apostle Paul was a pragmatic evangelist? If so, how did this shape his responses to situations in the early churches?

2. How should we interpret Paul's statement that he did not permit a woman "to teach or to have authority over a man" (1 Tim. 2:12)?

3. Overall, do Paul's practical instructions on head-coverings, orderly worship, and the church crisis at Ephesus seem reasonable and fair to you? Why or why not?

4. Do you think Paul ever conceded certain assumptions, or appealed to certain prejudices, of the people he was trying to persuade? If so, was his behavior compatible with the full inspiration of Scripture?

5. Is male leadership God's permanent will for male-female relationships? Why or why not?

CHAPTER 9

The Long Journey
Back to Eden

WOMEN IN CHRISTIAN HISTORY

Rain and snowfall from the highlands of western Turkey eventually find their way down to the Aegean Sea. A large part of this freshwater is carried by the Meander River, which patiently loops around mountains, through a fertile valley, and past ruined sites of ancient Christianity. The river definitely does not run in a straight line. There are obstacles to its progress—hills and rocks, and sometimes human interventions—and so, to use the word this river bequeathed to the English language, it *meanders*. It does not move as the crow flies, or as a Roman aqueduct might bear it. It sees lots of scenery. But the pull of gravity on the water is relentless as it travels toward the seacoast near Ephesus. The only questions concern the precise route it will follow and how long it may take to get to its destination.

The trajectory of the Spirit is like the Meander River. Historically, the healing of gender has not moved ahead in a straight line. Unfortunately, the Spirit has encountered all sorts of human obstacles in its way—deceptive ideologies, entrenched power structures, undercurrents of self-preservation, and even some stubborn hearts. At times it seems to the discouraged observer as though the river has turned back and is actually flowing the wrong way. But however ambiguous its direction may appear in the short term, the Spirit is headed in the right direction overall, and its final destination is certain. Through the long history of the church, slow and meandering progress continues to the present, as the Spirit faithfully draws the church toward an ever-fuller realization of its destiny—to return to what we once were, and in returning to become more like God.

Christianity has been a positive movement in history. No other religion or ideology can match its track record for compassion, intellectual enlightenment, support for the arts, the cultivation of science and technology, medical breakthroughs, liberty and justice, and overall civilizing influence. Nonetheless, as a sociocultural movement, it has had, and continues to have, flaws. Critics rightly denounce its lowpoints, like the Crusades, the Inquisition, and Christian complicity in anti-Semitism through the years. It has been too common for Christians to behave in ways that contradict the spirit and example of their founder and Lord. Ultimately this is because Christianity is a movement comprised of fallen human beings like ourselves.

Yet the church is not just a community of fallen human beings. It is also the temple of the Holy Spirit, and his presence and guidance is the other reality in all of this. As a result of the Spirit's presence, like a treasure in an earthen pot, the church has been an unmatched wellspring of truth, goodness, and beauty. Through the ministries of its members, humanity has been dignified, the cause of the powerless championed, sufferers consoled, hostilities pacified and enemies reconciled, and acts of self-sacrificing love have given hope to those in despair. The gospel has been proclaimed with clarity and lived with integrity, giving the world help to face life with courage and death with confidence. From the establishment of schools and universities, to hospitals and social welfare, the influence of the church has been powerfully felt. The issue is not whether Christianity has been helpful at all, but whether Christianity needs to be even *more* helpful than it has been to this point. With this in mind, we now consider the perception and place of women in the history of the church.

Backward Steps by the Fathers

Christianity underwent massive changes during its first five centuries. It began as a sect of Judaism, grew amid persecution to become the established religion of the Roman Empire, and eventually held on amid the decline and fall of that empire. Simultaneously the church evolved

from a freewheeling charismatic movement to an increasingly central-
ized organization. Perhaps inevitably, the church staked out its doctrinal contours and definitions of heresy, established its canon of
authoritative Scripture, and spelled out in no uncertain terms who was
in charge of the faith's expanding presence. Eventually the City of God,
as Augustine labeled what God was building amid the ruination of the
Roman Empire, would be identified with the multinational ecclesiastical corporation under construction. In retooling for its own long-
term survival, the church increasingly adopted the power-conscious
hierarchical patterns of its host cultures.

Already by the middle of the third century AD, charismatic phenomena receded (at least temporarily) into the background,[1] and
priests (the new custodians of the religion) had gained ascendancy
over the prophets in the church. Simply by designating its ministers
as priests, the church regressed back to an Old Testament model that
privileged males. But there was more than just this going on. In a pattern we will see repeated in future centuries, the move from a period
of spiritual renewal to institutional consolidation invariably shifted
focus from God's initiative to human enterprise, and with that a switch
back from gender equality to renewed male privilege.

The historical record of these early centuries reveals an intriguing
diversity in the church with respect to gender freedom. In places
women appear to have been priests and possibly even, in rare
instances, bishops.[2] Nonetheless, it was overall the age of the *Fathers*,
not the Mothers, and the seeds of this patriarchal pattern were sown
early on by venerated leaders like Irenaeus, Tertullian, Clement of
Alexandria, Origen, and, a bit later, Augustine of Hippo.[3]

Christian men tried very hard to resist the temptations of pagan
sexual immorality, and this struggle only intensified when celibacy
was adopted as the superior state for those in leadership. Women, the
objects of their sublimated desires, were viewed as potential seduc-
tresses. In time this drew Christian males to revisit the story of the
fall and there to "see" Eve, the archetypal woman, as the dangerous
temptress of Adam. And so Tertullian, counseling women on modest
attire, lashed out: "You are the Devil's gateway, you are the unsealer of

that forbidden tree, you are the first deserter of divine law; you are she who persuaded him who the Devil was not valiant enough to attack. You destroyed so easily God's image, man."[4] The Devil's gateway? Tertullian reflects the kind of thinking we encountered among Jewish rabbis and then heard echoed in Paul's own tongue-in-cheek, rabbinic-style comment in 1 Corinthians 11:7.

Later the great Augustine expressed similar sentiments. The Devil, he suggested, "first tried his deceit upon the woman, making his assault upon the weaker part of that human alliance, that he might gradually gain the whole."[5] As a result, Augustine claimed, we should be able to recognize that "there is a natural order observed among men, that women should serve men, and children their parents, because it is just that the weaker mind should serve the stronger."[6] Some resistance movements arose against this dominant trend, as evidenced by literature including *The Acts of Thecla* and *The Gospel of Mary Magdalene*. These were more empowering for women, and more insistent on a decisive break with the social divisions of mainstream society. But such literature and movements were marginalized by those positioned to define orthodoxy and maintain the status quo.

The impulse toward gender equality, however, which we attribute to the Spirit of God, cannot be suppressed. It finds ways to circumvent restrictions and creatively burst through. The pursuit of a deeper spirituality was one of those circumventing paths. Macrina, the saintly sister of Cappadocian theologian Gregory of Nyssa, profoundly influenced the latter's understanding of gender issues. Through the pursuit of a transcendent spirituality, Gregory later taught, women could escape the "inferiority" that attached to their physical side and refine the pure image of God within them. This dualistic assumption required that saintly women sublimate their femaleness, but the compensation was that they acquired a spiritual authority and prophetic stature to which even the greatest kings and popes occasionally deferred. The monastic tradition did not dislodge patriarchy from the church, by any means, but it did serve, within limits, as a means of female empowerment.

A Shocking Ceiling

The Sistine Chapel, the jewel of the Vatican in Rome, is one of the most sacred and beautiful places in the world. Awestruck visitors willingly stand for long periods of time to soak up the dazzling art that adorns its walls and ceiling. Michelangelo's sixteenth-century "The Last Judgment" covers the massive front wall of the chapel, enthralling observers with its vivid depiction of the eternal consequences of being finally chosen or rejected by Christ.

If you lean back and look up, you will see high above you a famous series of paintings of scenes from Genesis, arranged along the ceiling center-pole. The most famous of these depicts the creation of Adam by a white-bearded male deity. Their two arms are extended (God's powerfully, and Adam's languidly), with their two index fingers touching just enough for a life-giving connection to take place.

Michelangelo's portrayal of the fall is a couple of panels further along. The beguiling serpent is wound around a tree as it tempts Eve, and here is the shocker: the upper half of its body is not serpentine, but rather the head and naked torso of a *woman*! So on the previous panel, God is a man; on this one, the Devil is a woman. This visual image of the serpent, which predates Michelangelo, is obviously not biblical, but it does show how deep sexism runs in traditional Christian thought.[7] In the Sistine Chapel, where Catholic cardinals solemnly gather to select each new pope, the serpent has been portrayed this way for centuries now, and no one bothers to complain much about it.

What Happened in the Middle Ages

There are reasons why such thinking flourished in the centuries prior to Michelangelo. The tendency toward institutionalization that began in the age of the church fathers reached its zenith in the European vision of Christendom—wherein all of society, culture, and government were ruled by the church in a new and now *Holy* Roman Empire. The church adopted a secular organizational model and developed an elaborate pyramid of power and tight controls on access to authority. And a great deal of energy was invested in the contest between church and state over who should ultimately rule society.

Thomas Aquinas placed his personal stamp on the theology of Christendom. Like many Christian leaders before him, Aquinas believed in female inferiority, and said so. If anything, he actually worsened the Christian assumption of female inferiority by suggesting that the woman was *pervasively* defective—in body, will, and mind. Not surprisingly, Aquinas affirmed social hierarchy and a male priesthood. For him the ordination of women was unthinkable.

On the other side of the ledger, the cult of Mary the mother of God gathered strength. It is not a stretch to see that Christian devotion to Mary, which reached unprecedented levels in medieval Europe, was an intuitive (but ultimately misguided) attempt to compensate for the male perception of God promoted by the church. But even here the Spirit's impulse toward gender equity was thwarted by the particular persona of Mary so diligently cultivated by the establishment. Rather than the feisty Mary of Luke's gospel (Luke 1:46–55), medieval Christians were introduced to a sexless, serene, and passively suffering woman whose grace under affliction was promoted as an example to all—especially other women.

Beginning in the patristic period, women were permitted to choose the monastic path to spiritual perfection. In some ways the holy life offered an empowering escape from traditional roles of wife and mother. And therein lay an opportunity for the talent and giftedness of women to break through. The monasteries for women were an independent sphere in which women could develop administrative skills, exercise fiscal responsibility, devote themselves to learning, and earn public credibility and affection by serving human need. The leaders of these monastic centers were abbesses, and over time the exceptional among them developed great reputations for leadership and sagacity.

It is a popular misconception that the Middle Ages *were* the Dark Ages, and all was chaos, brutality, bovine ignorance, and plague for a thousand years. Rather, there was in this long age the same ebb and flow of spiritual vitality that has characterized the Christian faith from its founding. The so-called high Middle Ages (950–1350 AD) were such a time of spiritual renewal. An invigorated Christian faith expressed itself in a flowering of theology and the arts, the founding of universities, the building of great cathedrals, achievements of political unification, and, woven through all of this, a sincere passion for evangelism.[8]

Within this pervasive spirit of renewal, female orders produced some remarkable mystics whose writings continue to enrich the Christian tradition today. These mystics include Hildegaard of Bingen, Mechthild of Magdenberg, and Julian of Norwich. They offer some of our first substantive glimpses of the unique female Christian perspective. Mysticism's characteristic detachment from ordinary life and its focus on the inner, subjective world were natural matches for the limits within which these gifted women were obliged to live out their days. Male church leaders eventually conceded what popular piety more readily acknowledged—that real saints, regardless of gender, have a self-authenticating authority that cannot be discredited.

The Priesthood of *All* Believers

Like Augustine and Aquinas before them, the Reformers Martin Luther and John Calvin remained hierarchical in their understanding of gender relations. According to Luther, female subordination was the result of woman's sin, and an enduring biblical law. Calvin was more severe: female subordination had been built into the creation order from the very start. Calvin bought the old idea that Eve was Adam's subordinate helper, as well as Paul's rabbinic arguments for gender hierarchy (that is, Adam was born first, and Eve was deceived first). For the Reformers, these theological principles precluded women from teaching in public or exercising leadership over men. John Knox, a disciple of Calvin and founder of Scottish Presbyterianism, wrote *The First Blast of the Trumpet Against the Monstrous Regiment of Women* (1558) to decry the moral outrage of female rulers.

The Reformation was partly a step backward for women, inasmuch as the religious orders that had empowered some Roman Catholic women were suppressed. On the other hand, marriage was now preferred to celibacy, and both Luther and Calvin took wives themselves. Clearly such Reformers could not regard the expression of sexuality as evil or second-best. Logically, the female sex could no longer be viewed primarily as bait to hook and ruin godly men. A window was opening for Christian women to aspire to godliness without having to deny who they were. The Reformers also spoke glowingly of human love as a reflection of divine love, and in a number of significant ways espoused caring, bilateral dynamics for the marriage relationship.

Perhaps the greatest breakthrough for women came as a result of the Protestant emphasis on Bible reading by *all* Christians. The Reformers were convinced that the Bible had self-authenticating power, and they were passionate about getting this transforming Word out to the people. As long as the Bible was accessible only in Latin, the arcane language of the elite, the power of knowledge could be controlled. But the Protestant effort to translate the Scriptures into the vernacular languages of Europe changed all that. By following up translation work with the promotion of education and literacy for everyone, regardless of gender, the Reformation empowered women to an unprecedented degree.

Men and women moved forward together into what communications guru Marshall MacLuhan called (in honor of the inventor of the printing press) the Gutenberg galaxy. Education and literacy had been cultivated in the past among nuns in monasteries. But never before had such privileges been extended to the female population *as a whole*. Being able to read gave Protestant women direct, unmediated access to the things of God. It opened up an entire new world of ideas, and it allowed them, significantly, to begin thinking for themselves.

Finally, the Reformers celebrated the doctrine of the priesthood of *all* believers. No longer was access to God and his grace mediated through the narrow conduit of a human priesthood, with all the potential for unwholesome control that such an arrangement possessed. The newly recovered biblical principle of the priesthood of *all* believers (1 Peter 2:5, 9) was, by contrast, latently inclusive and egalitarian. It meant not only that every Christian could approach God directly with her needs for grace and guidance, but also that she could turn around and minister to others from the abundance she had received. In principle, then, access to God and empowerment to minister were gender-transparent and free.

Unfortunately, the magisterial Reformers did not *fully* grasp the implications of their own theological breakthrough. During their lifetimes they did not implement all that this biblical doctrine implied. This insight was grasped more firmly among certain Anabaptist groups on the so-called radical fringes of the Reformation. Overall, these Anabaptist groups, along with the English groups that followed them, placed greater stress on personal freedom before God, and were more suspicious of hierarchical authority. Because they were already disconnected from the social establishment, they were less tethered to its hierarchical conventions.

History, it is said, is written by winners, and there is a tendency in official church history-writing to dismiss the radical Reformation as an unimportant sideshow. But Christians, of all people, should never despise "the day of small things" (Zech. 4:10 KJV). In the language of Scripture, God chose "the lowly things of this world and the despised things—and the things that are not—to nullify the things that are" (1 Cor. 1:28). Sometimes the Spirit speaks most clearly from the margins. It is interesting how many emphases of the radical Reformers, like believers' baptism and the principle of separation of church and state, were eventually adopted by North American Christians.

Evangelicalism Arises and Responds

Evangelicalism as a movement has held to the central convictions of the Reformation and has drawn vitality from a series of large-scale spiritual awakenings, particularly in the English-speaking world over the past three centuries. Evangelistic in orientation and activist in ethos, the evangelical community has always been at the forefront of global Protestant missionary enterprise. And many of the roots of modern Christian feminism are to be found within the locus of this vibrant historic tradition.

Early nineteenth-century industrialization brought a restructuring of the traditional division of labor. Although patriarchy had always prevailed, there had been a fair measure of mutual participation on family farms and in small businesses. But with the advent of factories and mass production, husbands began leaving the house to earn a living in the outside world, while their wives stayed behind to raise families. A new vision for gender roles and family life developed which glorified motherhood and identified the home as the quintessential female sphere.

Then a very curious thing happened. "Nineteenth-century America reversed the traditional view of women as prone to sin in the image of Eve. Women were seen not as morally and spiritually inferior to men, but as superior."[9] It was as though women, having been excluded from the hurly-burly of public life, were granted the consolation prize of being regarded as the moral and religious superiors of men. Holiness, prayer, and good works were spiritual disciplines for which women were considered especially well-suited.

Patriarchy was not dismantled, though, and because of this Christians lived with a huge paradox: women were morally and spiritually superior, but still needed to be submissive and obedient to men.[10] Even if such inconsistent thinking persisted, this development was huge, for the historic assumption of woman's moral and spiritual inferiority had begun to weaken. Since then, most Christians defending gender hierarchy have been obliged to defend their position on grounds other than traditional belief in the moral and spiritual defectiveness of women.

Nineteenth-century evangelical men were prepared to defer to women as their spiritual superiors, as long as women agreed to be content with the limited opportunities their assigned station afforded. This was the trade-off—the negotiated settlement, if you will. Subsequently, the concept of women's proper "spiritual sphere" expanded beyond the hospitable home and the catechizing of children. It retained its identity as a spiritual sphere, but it broadened out. Awakened nineteenth-century religious enthusiasm in Britain and America was channeled into a myriad of voluntary societies, designed to address a remarkable range of social needs. Evangelical women created time for these endeavors, and many of the emergent organizations were led by women.

Initially, men patronized such female societies as a kind of child's play, but in time the women involved in these enterprises earned grudging admiration for their entrepreneurial vision, financial stability, and successful achievements. A voluntary society was not a church, so none of the restrictions and inhibitions related to clergy and ordination applied. Women were free to do their thing, and as it turned out they did it exceedingly well.

Women as Effective Missionaries

Awakened nineteenth-century evangelicalism was eager to take the gospel to the regions beyond. Female missionaries, both married and single, figured large in the movement from early on. Whenever world evangelization is the church's central focus, pragmatism prevails over minor doctrinal quibbles, and the enlistment of ever-greater numbers of female missionaries continued through the century. It has been estimated that by 1900 fully two-thirds of missionaries were women. The larger burden of world evangelization has always been carried, and continues to be carried, by women.[11]

Missionary endeavor was an exhilarating challenge, and women surprised the skeptics by their fortitude and ability in some of the most difficult situations on earth. One such pioneer was Charlotte "Lottie" Moon, who had a distinguished career in China from 1873 to 1912 before dying of starvation in that country. She once wrote: "What women want who come to China is free opportunity to do the largest possible work. . . . What women have a right to demand is perfect equality."[12] Ironically, Moon is probably still the most famous, and perhaps effective, of all Southern Baptist missionaries. Grudging critics conceded that while such women were overreaching their God-ordained stations in life, a case might be made for tolerating such impropriety for the sake of a greater good—the salvation of souls who would otherwise be eternally lost.

One of the most significant consequences of all this activity on the part of evangelical women was their emerging sense of self. As Barbara Welter has commented, "The doctor who treated two hundred patients a day . . . and the itinerant preacher who spoke until midnight and was off in her [rickshaw] at dawn, felt herself necessary and important."[13] From such successful experiences in spiritual ministry, which now extended beyond the home to the four corners of the globe, evangelical women grew in confidence.

The Holiness Movement and Pentecostalism

The Holiness movement, which began in the 1830s, provided another significant opportunity for Christian women to serve and lead, and eventually to place their stamp on America. The movement was interested in the perfection of the Christian's soul, and to this end its participants sought "entire sanctification." But it also aspired beyond the region of privatized spirituality to see *society* perfected through a purging from every form of immorality, systemic evil, and injustice.

There was a great emphasis on the Holy Spirit's ministry, and wherever this is present in church history there tends to be greater openness to the full participation of women. Phoebe Palmer, for example, was a major player in the Holiness movement. In turn Palmer influenced the next generation of Holiness women, which included Catherine Booth, cofounder of the Salvation Army, and Methodist Frances Willard, who became president of the World's Woman's Christian Temperance Union. In the midst of their daunting responsibilities, Booth wrote *Female Ministry* (1859), an apologetic for women preachers, and Willard wrote *Women in the Pulpit* (1889), in which she pleaded for more gender-inclusive language in the church.

As the Holiness movement created new denominations, a high percentage of their ministers were women. The Church of the Nazarene, the largest of these, made ordination of women official policy in 1894, and Seth Rees, founder of the Pilgrim Holiness Church, commented that "no church that is acquainted with the Holy Ghost will object to the public ministry of women."[14] Oberlin College in Ohio, the flagship college of the movement, was also the first in America to accept women as students.

The vision of perfection shared by those who identified with the Holiness movement led them to engage a remarkable range of social challenges in America. Oberlin was one of the earliest centers of abolitionist sentiment, and the movement contributed significantly to changes in mid-nineteenth-century popular opinion about the compatibility of slavery with Christian morality. In time, Holiness women recognized the parallels between the racial oppression they fought and the gender oppression they continued to endure. In their emerging consciousness lay some important roots of modern feminism.

The Holiness crusade, for that is what it became, enlisted an army of people to feed the hungry, clothe the naked, alleviate suffering, get prostitutes off the street and children into orphanages, and promote human welfare generally. Its campaigns for legal changes took its members to the highest courts, and its compassion brought salvation to the slums of America's largest cities. The significant involvement of women in these various causes, from promoting women's suffrage to attacking alcohol abuse, provided proof, to their skeptics and themselves, of their strength and ability *as women*.

The modern Pentecostal movement, which began in an outbreak of tongues-speaking at a tiny Kansas Bible school in 1901, descended directly from the earlier Holiness movement. Much Holiness doctrine and practice was transported wholesale into Pentecostalism. Both movements placed great stress on a life-transforming "baptism in the Holy Spirit" experience, and both emphasized the Spirit as the key to empowered living and effective Christian service.

If anything, Pentecostalism was more thoroughly egalitarian than its predecessor. The International Church of the Foursquare Gospel was founded by Aimee Semple McPherson, a female evangelist from Canada. The Assemblies of God, which coalesced in 1916, is the largest denominational beneficiary of the Pentecostal impulse in global Christianity. It continues to be officially egalitarian, and cites fulfillment of Joel's egalitarian prophecy (Joel 2) on the day of Pentecost as a chief biblical basis for its position. For Pentecostals, Holy Spirit *charisma*, rather than gender or office, is the principal basis for, and supreme validation of, ministry.

Some other Christian churches have not been as ready to affirm the full equality of women in church and society. Even within churches with Holiness and Pentecostal heritages, there has been the occasional tendency to regress to less egalitarian practices. This often accompanies a growing preoccupation with structural issues, and sometimes reflects an unconscious desire for greater acceptance by the religious and cultural mainstream.

DIAGRAM 9.1. A Recurring Pattern in Christian History

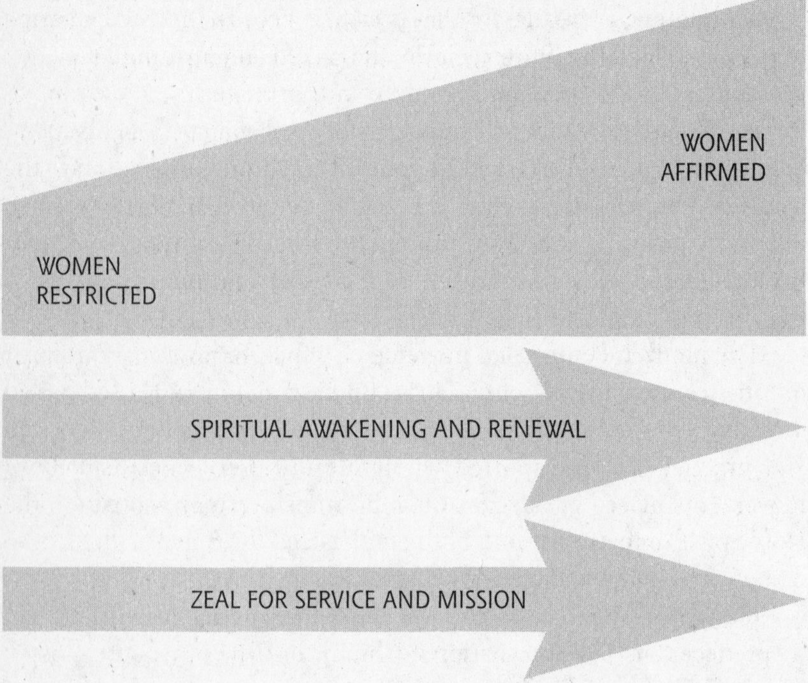

WOMEN
AFFIRMED

WOMEN
RESTRICTED

SPIRITUAL AWAKENING AND RENEWAL

ZEAL FOR SERVICE AND MISSION

Two things are consistently associated with welcoming women to participate as valued equals. One is a practical emphasis on the Holy Spirit, and the other is an enthusiasm for kingdom-building through evangelistic effort, benevolent ministry, and social reform. When the mission of the church is more important than the institution's internal power structures, women tend to be affirmed and commissioned. Such conditions have been the most fertile soil for egalitarian attitudes and practices. Consequently, those who long for significant improvements in the status of women should be praying for another major spiritual awakening among Christians.

The Contemporary Scene

Feminism promotes the full equality and unrestricted participation of women in church and society. There are basically two kinds today—

Christian and secular. Christian feminists are believers in Jesus who base their lives on his teachings and example. Secular feminists are those who give no significant place to Christ, but share with Christian feminists a commitment to promoting the full equality and dignity of women.

Christian feminists have been accused of buying into an alien secular agenda and capitulating to the ideological pressures of a godless world. But our brief historical review has shown that Christian feminism actually predated secular feminism. Indeed, the roots of secular feminism lie in the Christian movement itself, and particularly in its recent evangelical and Holiness traditions. It is no accident that secular feminism emerged from a cultural environment profoundly shaped by Christianity. Its vision of female empowerment and gender equality has Christian roots. Serious differences exist between the Christian and secular versions of feminism. But secular feminism is not some alien threat from the outside. It is Christianity's own wounded and estranged daughter.

Some people often erroneously assume that modern secular feminism began in the early 1960s. In fact, its roots go back to earlier developments in Christian history. Sarah and Angelina Grimké became leaders in the slavery abolition campaign and, in the process, scandalized traditionalists by frequently speaking to "promiscuous" (that is, gender-mixed) audiences. Through all of this the Grimké sisters retained an evangelical faith. It was a natural development for such women to feel not only sympathy for, but solidarity with victims of racism. The issue of women's rights became explicit in the efforts of a new generation of women leaders that included Lucretia Mott, Elizabeth Cady Stanton, and Susan B. Anthony. The work of these three giants eventually bore fruit in 1920 when the right of women to vote in America was granted.

At this point, *secular* feminism emerged. Even though most supporters of the women's rights movement were still evangelical Christians, Mott and Anthony preferred to avoid using explicitly Christian doctrine and language to advance their work. Stanton grew up Presbyterian and had a conversion of sorts under the influence of evangelist

Charles Finney. Later in her youth, she was turned off by a young preacher who, having been helped through seminary by financial contributions from the girls' club to which she belonged, subsequently expressed disdain for women.[15]

Eventually Stanton drifted into religious skepticism, having completely soured on the Christian faith over what she perceived as the foot-dragging of institutional Christianity on women's emancipation.[16] Because rigid biblical literalism remained so widespread among male clergy, and so few were able to detect the progressive motions of the Spirit to which the Scriptures bear witness, mainstream Protestantism drove some of its most gifted and idealistic daughters into a spiritual wasteland. Not only was Scripture discredited, but contact with many women was severed altogether.

Ironically, the Christianity that birthed modern feminism is now viewed by most feminists as a formidable engine of oppression *against* women. At root, secular feminism is a legitimate cry of the human spirit against the demeaning and dehumanizing treatment of women. It is justly outraged by circumstances God never meant to exist. Yet the tragedy of this movement is that it no longer looks to the triune God for help and inspiration, but instead has chosen to embrace the Enlightenment ideal of individual rights and the Darwinian concept of hostile struggle. These regrettable choices continue to undermine the very possibilities of gender mutuality and loving reciprocity for which men and women were designed.

Signs of Hope

When the Spirit is present in power, and Christians are intent on mission, there will always be wider spheres of opportunity and freedom for women. It is a sign of stagnation when a church turns inward, giving undue attention to structure, polity, and concerns over access to ecclesiastical power. Christian preoccupation with access to ordination may ultimately be misguided anyway, since clericalism (that is, clergy-centeredness) is itself a manifestation of the hierarchical, worldly approach to power that is passing away. The Roman Catholic Church, which claims over a billion adherents worldwide, complains of a crisis in recruiting celibate male clergy. At the same time, and with the blessing of Vatican II, the ranks and responsibilities of the Roman Catholic lay minister are increasing exponentially. Significantly, more than 80 percent of such lay ministers are now women.[17]

In China, the largest country on earth, the growth of the Christian faith has been proceeding for a half-century in the face of considerable hostility, and for the most part without the help of ordained clergy and the normal institutional support structures. Much of this Christian advance is taking place through unofficial house churches, and I am assured by regular visitors to China that the larger portion of these, especially in the rural areas, are led by women—often in their early twenties. One has to step back from such contemporary developments and ask: Are these mere quirks of history, or are they perhaps further signs of a faithful, irrepressible impulse of the Spirit of God? I am persuaded that such developments indeed witness to the movement of the Spirit. Because of the promises of God, and assurances such as these, we can look to the future with hope and expectation. Greater gender equality, freedom, and mutuality are most certainly ahead.

chapter summary

For two thousand years the church has struggled to follow the Holy Spirit's promptings toward the complete renewal of gender relations. Nevertheless, the liberating impulse of the Spirit keeps bursting forth, and history indicates that this is most noticeable when the people of God are experiencing spiritual renewal and involved in evangelistic advance. In the big picture, and despite some tragic regressions and estrangements along the way, the church is being patiently guided toward the goal of gender renewal. The Spirit's upward trajectory has been evident in recent centuries through the Reformation, the evangelical tradition, modern missionary enterprise, and the Holiness and Pentecostal movements. But best of all, there are reasons to hope for further progress just ahead. So come Holy Spirit!

Questions for Individual or Group Reflection

1. Describe the changes experienced by women in your family over the past several generations. Overall, have these been good or bad?

2. What do you consider the most positive developments regarding gender in the history of Christianity so far?

3. How have you, or Christian women you know, been affected by persistent hierarchical attitudes in the church?

4. Churches tend to be most open to the contributions of women when two conditions exist. What are those conditions?

5. In what sense is secular feminism Christianity's own "estranged daughter"? How might this perception of secular feminism affect our attitude toward feminists?

6. Have there been any gains for women that you think should be reversed? What further changes, if any, do you think still need to take place?

CHAPTER 10

Understanding the Times

a pivotal moment in history?

B e sure to see the statue," a friend urged as I headed off to a retreat center near Guelph, Ontario. "It's wonderful!" After a long, hectic day of travel, I finally located Loyola House in an exquisite, natural, spirit-calming setting. Time pretty much stopped. It was really, really quiet, because I had arrived during a rigorous thirty-day silent retreat. Participants were following Loyola's classic *Spiritual Exercises* as an aid to discerning God's guidance for their lives.

After a leisurely walk through woods and daffodils, I came upon the life-size bronze statue of Saint Ignatius the Pilgrim I had been told about. This Ignatius was clearly on a journey—as I stood there I felt his movement and progress. Hand clutched to his chest, he was leaning into a strong wind which whipped his cloak and flattened his robe against his skin. But it was Ignatius's face that I found most arresting. It was disciplined and intent, even tilted a bit to one side as he peered into the distance. He felt the wind, and was trying to move toward its source. For me, he was seeking to discern, and follow, the movement of the Spirit, the breath and wind of God. Ignatius the Pilgrim sums up more effectively than words the central theme of this book.

Where Have We Come?

We've been tracking the redemptive movement of God's Spirit through history to this point in time. We began with the biblical vision of the Trinity as a non-tiered fellowship of divine love, and then the creation of people to image God in their relationships as male and female.

Among its many tragic consequences, the fall produced gender alienation and oppression, evils which persist in many forms today. The incarnation was a great leap forward in the gender revolution, and Jesus Christ's attitude toward women still remains the highest revelation of God's heart and will on this issue.

Following Pentecost the early church made substantial progress toward gospel ideals, but certain vestiges of patriarchy persisted—due in part to the apostles' conscious strategy of accommodating the church's ideals to first-century social realities. Since then, the Holy Spirit's intent has been most honored in times of spiritual renewal, and most neglected during periods of institutional consolidation. A slowly ascending pattern of progress, offset by disappointing regressions, continues to the present, as the Spirit continues prodding the church toward a fuller realization of the ultimate goal—that our likeness to God should be fully restored.

We are still on this long journey back to the garden, and the relational renewal it symbolizes. Our return is proving to be an arduous one. Dynamics of gender oppression are deeply ingrained in this fallen world. From a global perspective, women continue to suffer all manner of troubles, from female infanticide to domestic violence, and from slave-labor to the insidious silencing of their voice.

We have rejoiced over instances of progress. But whenever gains are made, it seems, oppression mutates into some other virulent form. In Western societies, for example, women have obtained the right to vote, to attend university, and to some legal equality before the law. All this has been positive. But now women also must function in an environment in which cohabitation without commitment is normalized, where popular culture objectifies and sexualizes women rather than treating them as persons, where only "superwomen" can succeed in careers while still carrying a disproportionate responsibility for children and home, and where the typical single parent is a woman below the poverty line. Few women want to go back to the older oppressive patterns and expectations; there is little nostalgia for those bygone days. But the newer faces of gender oppression are disturbing.

Where Real Change Must Begin

At best, the unaided history of humanity itself invites only modest expectations. Only a supernatural intervention, or a series of such interventions, can shake things up and produce anything substantively better than what we have now. But our hope is that with God all things are possible. Fortunately, he has intervened and has promised more interventions to come. The most decisive of these so far was the incarnation of the Word, the Savior Jesus Christ, and with his arrival the inauguration of the kingdom of God on earth. Through Christ's coming a beachhead was established in hostile territory, and the foundations were laid for an alternative social order—one in which the will of God prevails and humans can reclaim their true humanity. The church of Jesus Christ was empowered by the Holy Spirit and left on earth to be a prototype of this coming kingdom. Its task is to show the world ahead of time what everything is someday going to look like, when God will finally have perfect dominion "from sea to sea" (Ps. 72:8).

The church is the body of Christ, the chief instrument through which his heart and will is worked out in the world today. Here now, the church is to *embody*, and not just announce, the good news. Lesslie Newbigin, a great twentieth-century missionary and vigorous champion of the uniqueness of Christ in an age of pluralism, has said: "The most important contribution which the Church can make to a new social order is to be itself a new social order."[1] And this new social order, because it breathes the spirit of its founder rather than the spirit of the world, will not be fixated on maintaining power and control (or addicted to the literature of leadership), but instead will be characterized by the new-order values of mutual respect, self-giving service, reciprocal affirmation, and encouragement of all.

To Everything There Is a Season

Parts of the world today, like the Mediterranean world of the first century, may not yet be ready for the truth of women's complete liberation in Christ. If in these areas the church should demand at once "the whole enchilada" of women's inheritance rights in Christ, it would only make evangelism difficult to impossible. When the realities of a culture are stridently resistant to social change, redemptive Christians may judiciously have to settle for restraining the more excessive abuses of hierarchy in that context. The good news is that numerous New Testament instructions can be applied directly to such situations, given this was the church's strategy in New Testament times.

Nevertheless, the church cannot afford to be complacent in its strategic short-term compromises. It should always be pressing toward a fuller realization of Scripture's redemptive vision. Whenever there is the smallest door through which to move forward, the church should seize the opportunity. The church should be leading humanity, rather than bringing up the rear, in the struggle for deliverance from all the oppressive consequences of sin. This is all part of God's kingdom coming and the will of God being done on earth as it is in heaven.

Such a window of opportunity now exists in different parts of the world, especially in the West. In such places it is urgent that the church move ahead in a liberating direction. The cost of not doing so escalates daily. In these regions the perception that Christianity is enmeshed with patriarchy is now widely regarded as a valid reason for rejecting Jesus Christ. The credibility of the gospel is at stake.

Unfortunately, in many cases conservative Christianity is not a particularly healthy or empowering environment for women. Too often its ethos is not one in which they are encouraged to excel, to make full use of their abilities, or to become leaders. Recently I learned that a prominent evangelical church has an established practice of asking gifted female "directors" of ministries to leave pastoral staff meetings so that the male pastors can deliberate on the more important matters privately. Indeed, the proverbial glass ceiling can be very low in the sanctuary. Low self-esteem, pandemic among females in the West, is particularly serious among Christian girls and women. Too often churches foster among women traits of triviality, dependence on others, and general underdevelopment of the self.

We must realize—in a moment of painful epiphany, perhaps—how much the gospel of Jesus Christ is discredited by our continued affirmation of gender hierarchy. And we must appreciate the extent of the personal pain caused by the perpetuation of sexist attitudes and patriarchal structures. But change is also urgently needed for the welfare of the church itself. Without the voice of women in decision-making, and without adequate female representation in leadership roles, churches themselves are less than whole and much weaker than they were intended to be.

Grace-Filled Egalitarianism

Research is showing that egalitarian marriages tend generally to be happier and freer of abuse.[2] Nonetheless, even in the West, we believe, it can be acceptable for a Christian couple to decide (though mutually, of course) to maintain their marriage and home according to the pattern of male priority and leadership. Many Christian men, and some Christian women, still prefer such a traditional arrangement. Couples who opt for such a model can still experience great love and joy, and even find personal fulfillment. Softly hierarchical partnerships in ministry can be highly effective, and such relationships can be very winsome to some outsiders. These things should be above question.

The only caveat, and it is an important one, is that this traditional marriage model must be viewed as a matter of choice (by both partners) rather than a binding biblical obligation. It is acceptable to perpetuate this kind of traditional marriage as long as both parties enter into it voluntarily, and the arrangement itself can periodically be reviewed. But it is unacceptable to claim that this is the only way, or even the best way, for Christian couples to relate. It must not be promoted as God's will for Christians and normative for all. Instead, the church should not only allow, but encourage others of its members to move further ahead in the direction of kingdom ideals. The church should welcome, rather than discourage, those who are prepared to move beyond cultural conventions to embrace a more excellent way.

It's time for greater desegregation of adult ministries. Ministry to men does not always have to be about golf tournaments, paintball, and steak-outs. Ministry to women does not need to consistently involve fancy luncheons, esteem-building seminars, and cosmetic demonstrations. Churches that move toward more desegregation will discover that women and men who respect each other as equals have more in common than just a shared desire to rekindle marital romance.

Beyond domestic arrangements women should be encouraged, just as men always have been, to seek the greatest opportunities to contribute to society and the larger spheres of service within the church. Of course, it is always contrary to God's purposes, regardless of whether one is male or female, to aspire to a position of church leadership in a competitive, self-aggrandizing way. Women are just as doomed as men to failure in ministry if they are driven like that; no one should fight too aggressively to be a shepherd. Divine calling, Holy Spirit anointing, and adequate preparation, experience, gifts, and spirituality are still essential for any woman or man who aspires to church offices of leadership and service. The ministry requires so much self-giving love that one misses the mark to think of an office as an achievement. What has to change is the notion that female candidates are disqualified from, or unsuited for, the highest positions in society and the largest responsibilities in the family of God.

Children will continue to be important to Spirit-led couples, families, and churches. They will be celebrated as God's special gifts and given the highest priority by the men and women to whom they are related. God is the giver of life, and Christianity is life-affirming. Raising a new generation celebrates life and witnesses to hope. Careers are never to flourish at the expense of neglecting vulnerable family members. But the revolutionary dimension for Christians is that fathers will be intimately involved, alongside mothers, as *equal partners* in the joys and responsibilities of raising a family.

Going with the Biblical Flow

This vision of gender relations grows out of the Scriptures. Our approach to interpreting the Bible pays careful attention to the Bible's inspired instructions for believers at previous times in history, and then seeks to discern the direction of the Spirit as he leads us into the future. This will always be consistent with the movement already discerned in the Bible, but will extrapolate this vector out beyond the culturally accommodated practices of the early church itself.

This progressive approach to Scripture requires a paradigm shift for those who have grown accustomed to a static hermeneutic. And paradigm shifts are never easy! It is important to keep in mind that the Holy Spirit is still at work in the church to guide her into all truth. As the godly Puritan leader John Robinson once famously declared, "The Lord hath more truth and light yet to break forth from his holy word." The canon of Scripture is complete, but our understanding of its inspired message continues to develop. The message of women's full equality and freedom does not contradict the Bible. Just the opposite— it expresses an important aspect of its liberating message. To embrace gender equality and freedom is not to discredit Scripture, but to honor its true intent.

What about Homosexuality?

Some readers will understandably be concerned that such an approach to Scripture could undermine Scripture's absolute truth claims and lead down a slippery slope to unbiblical beliefs and behaviors, including homosexual practice. The concern is a legitimate one. Some people lump together the contemporary quests for racial, gender, and homosexual rights as one, and argue that each of these is consistent with the impulses of God's Spirit.

Those who subscribe honestly to the authority of Scripture must always object to such a claim. Chronological "movement" in Scripture signals that the Spirit is leading the church on a trajectory toward a higher, more settled ethical stance. This is the case with respect to slavery and women's equality. But in the case of homosexual practice no such movement can be discerned. From the Pentateuch to Paul, the Bible consistently and unequivocally condemns homosexual practice as wrong. In this instance there is no movement and there is no trajectory.

Some readers will no doubt judge parts of this book to be less than airtight. Admittedly, some of the ideas put forward are not yet perfectly developed, and some legitimate questions may persist. Nonetheless, very few readers wish for a return to the way women were treated in Old Testament times—being sold by their brothers, divorced on a whim, and dropped off in the harems of powerful men. Most will also agree that granting women the right to vote and giving them access to higher education were steps in the right direction. So however much critics may object to certain particulars of this book, I hope that they will agree that there *is* a progressive movement of the Spirit afoot in history, and our duty as Christians is to align ourselves with it as best we can.

A Pivotal Moment of Opportunity

Progressively through history the Spirit has been guiding the church into all truth. Different doctrines have had their special times at center stage and been the focus of concentrated attention. The doctrines of Christ, the Trinity, and the canon of Scripture were hammered out in the first centuries of Christianity, and orthodox views of humanity and sin during the fifth-century Pelagian controversies. The meaning of the atonement was gradually clarified from the eleventh century onward, and justification by faith was illuminated by the Reformers in the sixteenth, and so forth. The great thing is that these gains have been more or less cumulative.[3] This may well be the historic moment for the people of God finally to affirm without equivocation the genuine biblical vision of gender equality, freedom, and mutuality. I can certainly visualize my great-aunt Mary Slessor, the pioneer missionary to Africa, and others like her in the great cloud of witnesses, urging us to go for it.

In the thirteenth century, the Venetian Polo brothers returned to Italy after one of their epic expeditions to the Far East. They brought back letters from Kublai Khan, the Mongol emperor of China, inviting the pope to send missionaries to introduce Christianity to the great land he ruled from Beijing. Unfortunately, Rome's response was halfhearted and ultimately ineffectual. A strategic opportunity was squandered.

Six hundred years later, European colonial powers imposed their wills (and their opium) on the Chinese government and demanded that their citizens be free to enter China's interior without harassment. The legitimacy of what the European powers did during those infamous Opium Wars was clearly questionable. Nevertheless, an English couple named Hudson and Maria Taylor discerned an opportunity for the advance of Christ's more peaceable kingdom. They, and the intrepid women and men of the China Inland Mission, seized that moment to do something unprecedented in history.

The results, as they say, are still coming in. Despite intervening years of oppressive Communist rule, mainland China may soon have more Christians than any other nation on earth. And the empowered Chinese church now has its own vision for a great evangelistic campaign westward through Muslim lands all the way back to Jerusalem—one to be led this time by suffering servants rather than crusaders. These are amazing developments. Very possibly, however, they're happening much later—600 years later, in fact—than they needed to. How different the entire course of world history might have been. The lesson seems clear: When a strategic opportunity arises, Christians need to seize the day.

With respect to gender relations, this finally may be the opportune moment to implement the vision toward which the Spirit has always been pointing. These times in which we live can bewilder us, for we live in an age much like one a great Victorian described—one in which the noise of things passing away still drowns out the sound of the things that are coming to be. Yet new things *are* coming to be. There definitely *is* movement. Along with an ability to discern this fresh wind we may also need a dose of sanctified daring. God is up to something really big and we can have the joy and satisfaction of being part of it.

Questions for Individual or Group Reflection

1. How would greater participation by women enhance your church's ministry? Or perhaps be detrimental to it?

2. Where have you observed women today fully exercising spiritual gifts?

3. In what ways is the gospel good news for women?

Resources for Further Study

France, R. T. *Women in the Church's Ministry: A Test Case for Biblical Interpretation*. Grand Rapids, Mich.: Eerdmans, 1995.

Giles, Kevin. *The Trinity and Subordinationism: The Doctrine of God and the Contemporary Gender Debate*. Downers Grove, Ill.: InterVarsity, 2002.

Groothuis, Rebecca. *Good News for Women: A Biblical Picture of Gender Equality*. Grand Rapids, Mich.: Baker, 1997.

Keener, Craig. *Paul, Women, and Wives: Marriage and Women's Ministry in the Letters of Paul*. Peabody, Mass.: Hendrickson, 1992.

Kroeger, Catherine Clark, and Mary Evans, eds. *The IVP Women's Bible Commentary*. Downers Grove, Ill.: InterVarsity, 2001.

MacHaffie, Barbara. *Her Story: Women in Christian Tradition*. Philadelphia: Fortress, 1986.

Marshall, I. Howard. *Beyond the Bible: Moving from Scripture to Theology*. Grand Rapids, Mich.: Baker, 2004.

Pierce, Ronald, Rebecca Groothuis, and Gordon Fee, eds. *Discovering Biblical Equality: Complementarity Without Hierarchy*. Downers Grove, Ill.: InterVarsity, 2004.

Ruether, Rosemary Radford. *Women and Redemption: A Theological History*. Minneapolis: Fortress, 1998.

Tucker, Ruth, and Walter Liefield. *Daughters of the Church: Women and Ministry from New Testament Times to the Present*. Grand Rapids, Mich.: Zondervan, 1987.

Webb, William. *Slaves, Women, and Homosexuals: Exploring the Hermeneutics of Cultural Analysis*. Downers Grove, Ill.: InterVarsity, 2001.

Notes

Introduction

1. James Buchan, *The Expendable Mary Slessor* (New York: Seabury, 1980).
2. Mary Pipher, *Reviving Ophelia: Saving the Selves of Adolescent Girls* (New York: Putnam, 1994).

Chapter 1: Tracing the Trajectory of the Spirit

1. Hans Küng, *My Struggle for Freedom* (Grand Rapids, Mich.: Eerdmans, 2003), 306.
2. John Eldredge, *Wild at Heart: Discovering the Secrets of a Man's Soul* (Nashville: Thomas Nelson, 2001).
3. Craig Blomberg and James Beck, eds., *Two Views on Women in Ministry* (Grand Rapids, Mich.: Zondervan, 2001).
4. John Piper and Wayne Grudem, eds., *Recovering Biblical Manhood and Womanhood* (Wheaton, Ill: Crossway, 1991), 32–35.
5. William Webb, *Slaves, Women, and Homosexuals: Exploring the Hermeneutics of Cultural Analysis* (Downers Grove, Ill.: InterVarsity, 2001).
6. Glen G. Scorgie, "Hermeneutics and the Meditative Use of Scripture: The Case for a Baptized Imagination," *Journal of the Evangelical Theological Society* 44, no. 2 (June 2001): 271–84.
7. N. T. Wright, *The New Testament and the People of God* (Minneapolis: Fortress, 1992), 139–44.
8. Webb, *Slaves, Women, and Homosexuals*, 256.
9. Paul Hanson, *The Diversity of Scripture: A Theological Interpretation* (Philadelphia: Fortress, 1982), 105.

Chapter 2: God Before All Things

1. Paul Jewett, *God, Creation, and Revelation* (Grand Rapids, Mich.: Eerdmans, 1991), 324.
2. C. S. Lewis, *Mere Christianity* (London: Fontana, 1955), 147.
3. A. W. Tozer, *The Knowledge of the Holy* (San Francisco: Harper & Row, 1961), 9.
4. Roger Olson and Chris Hall, *The Trinity* (Grand Rapids, Mich.: Eerdmans, 2002), ch. 1.
5. Tertullian, *Apology*, 21, in *Ante-Nicene Fathers*, vol. 3.

6.　See Kevin Giles, *The Trinity and Subordinationism* (Downers Grove, Ill.: InterVarsity, 2002).

7.　Augustine, *On the Trinity*, 1.14, in *Nicene and Post-Nicene Fathers*, 1st series, vol. 3.

8.　J. N. D. Kelly, *The Athanasian Creed* (New York and Evanston, Ill.: Harper & Row, 1964), 19.

9.　Second Helvetic Confession, ch. 3; quoted by Giles, *The Trinity and Subordinationism*, 59.

10.　Millard Erickson, *Christian Theology*, 2nd ed. (Grand Rapids, Mich.: Baker, 1998), 789–90.

11.　Gilbert Bilezikian, "Hermeneutical Bungee-Jumping: Subordination in the Godhead," *Journal of the Evangelical Theological Society* 40, no. 1 (March 1997): 57–68.

12.　John Calvin, *Institutes of the Christian Religion*, 2 vols., ed. J. McNeill (Philadelphia: Westminster, 1960), 1.13.26.

13.　Giles, *The Trinity and Subordinationism*, 198.

14.　Wayne Grudem, "Appendix 1: The Meaning of *Kephale*," in *Recovering Biblical Manhood and Womanhood*, eds. John Piper and Wayne Grudem (Wheaton, Ill.: Crossway, 1991), 457.

15.　Millard Erickson, *God in Three Persons* (Grand Rapids, Mich.: Baker, 1995), 331.

Chapter 3: Created to Be Like God

1.　John Calvin, *Institutes of the Christian Religion*, 2 vols., ed. J. McNeill (Philadelphia: Westminster, 1960), 1.14.2.

2.　Huston Smith, *The World's Religions* (San Francisco: Harper, 1991), 281.

3.　C. S. Lewis, *The Weight of Glory, And Other Addresses* (New York: Macmillan, 1949), 15.

4.　Emil Brunner, *Man in Revolt: A Christian Anthropology*, trans. Olive Wyon (Philadelphia: Westminster, 1947), 92.

5.　Ibid., 106.

6.　Karl Barth, *Church Dogmatics*, 3.1 (Edinburgh: T. & T. Clark, 1958), 183.

7.　Walter Brueggemann, *Genesis* (Atlanta: John Knox, 1982), 11.

Chapter 4: What Went Wrong

1.　See Raymond Ortlund, "Male-Female Equality and Male Headship: Genesis 1–3," in *Recovering Biblical Manhood and Womanhood*, eds. John Piper and Wayne Grudem (Wheaton, Ill.: Crossway, 1991), 95–112.

2. Kevin Giles, *The Trinity and Subordinationism* (Downers Grove, Ill.: InterVarsity, 2002), 10.

3. Ronald Youngblood, *The Book of Genesis*, 2nd ed. (Grand Rapids, Mich.: Baker, 1991), 52.

4. Aida Bensacon Spencer, *Beyond the Curse: Women Called to Ministry* (Nashville: Thomas Nelson, 1985).

5. Alice Mathews, "The Theological Is Also Personal: The 'Place' of Evangelical Protestant Women in the Church," in *Theological Literacy in the Twenty-first Century*, ed. Rodney Petersen (Grand Rapids, Mich.: Eerdmans, 2002), 143.

Chapter 5: An Age of Patriarchy

1. Phyllis Trible, *Texts of Terror* (Philadelphia: Fortress, 1984).

2. Stanley Grenz and Denise Kjesbo, *Women in the Church* (Downers Grove, Ill.: InterVarsity, 1995), 167.

3. Walther Eichrodt, *Theology of the Old Testament*, 2 vols., trans. J. A. Baker (Philadelphia: Westminster, 1961), 1:381–91.

4. *Babylonian Talmud*, Hagiga 16b.

5. Ibid., Hagiga 3a.

6. *Jerusalem Talmud*, Sota 3.4.

7. *Mishnah*, Abot 1.5.

8. *Babylonian Talmud*, Sabbat 33b.

9. Josephus, *Jewish Antiquities*, 4.8.15.

10. Philo, *On the Embassy to Gaius*, 40 (319).

11. Philo, *On the Creation*, 59 (165).

12. *Mishnah*, Horayot 3.7.

13. Josephus, *Against Apion*, 2.25.

14. Philo, *Questions and Answers on Genesis*, 1.33.

15. Ibid., 1.43.

16. *Babylonian Talmud*, Menahot 43b.

17. R. T. France, *Women in the Church's Ministry* (Grand Rapids, Mich.: Eerdmans, 1995), 76.

Chapter 6: Jesus Christ and Women

1. Aida Bensancon Spencer, *Beyond the Curse* (Nashville: Nelson, 1985), 57–61.

2. Donald Kraybill, *The Upside-Down Kingdom* (Scottdale, Pa.: Herald Press, 1978).

3. Ben Witherington III, *Women and the Genesis of Christianity* (Cambridge: Cambridge University Press, 1990), chs. 4–7.

4. Paul Jewett, *Man as Male and Female* (Grand Rapids, Mich.: Eerdmans, 1975), 94.

5. Ibid., 103.

6. Spencer, *Beyond the Curse*, 55.

7. Quoted in Jewett, *Man as Male and Female*, 97.

8. Witherington, *Women and the Genesis of Christianity*, ch. 13.

9. H. Flender, quoted in Witherington, *Women and the Genesis of Christianity*, 201.

10. Roger Stronstad, *The Charismatic Theology of St. Luke* (Peabody, Mass.: Hendrickson, 1984).

11. Mary Daly, *Beyond God the Father* (Boston: Beacon, 1973), 19.

12. *The Koran*, trans. N. J. Dawood (London: Penguin, 1993), Sura 19.88.

13. Rosemary Radford Ruether, *Women and Redemption* (Minneapolis: Fortress, 1998), 277.

14. G. Beasley-Murray, *Gospel of Life: Theology in the Fourth Gospel* (Peabody, Mass.: Hendrickson, 1991), 118.

15. Sue Monk Kidd, *When the Heart Waits* (San Francisco: Harper San Francisco, 1990), 54.

Chapter 7: Gender in the Early Church

1. Mark Strauss, *Distorting Scripture? The Challenge of Bible Translation and Gender Accuracy* (Downers Grove, Ill.: InterVarsity, 1998), 147.

2. S. Singer, trans., *The Authorized Daily Prayer Book of the United Hebrew Congregations of the British Empire*, 6th ed. (London: Eyre & Spottiswoode, 1900), 5–6.

3. *Babylonian Talmud*, Hagiga 4a; cf. *Tosefta*, Berakot 6.18.

4. F. F. Bruce, *The Epistle to the Galatians* (Grand Rapids, Mich.: Eerdmans, 1982), 190.

5. William Mounce, *Analytical Lexicon to the Greek New Testament* (Grand Rapids, Mich.: Zondervan, 1993), 102.

6. Stanley Hauerwas and William Willimon, *Resident Aliens* (Nashville: Abingdon, 1989).

7. I. Howard Marshall, *1 Peter* (Downers Grove, Ill.: InterVarsity, 1991), 24–25.

8. Rebecca Groothuis, *Good News for Women: A Biblical Picture of Gender Equality* (Grand Rapids, Mich.: Baker, 1997), 175–76.

9. R. T. France, *Women in the Church's Ministry* (Grand Rapids, Mich.: Eerdmans, 1995), 83.

10. Ibid.

Chapter 8: Old Habits Die Hard

1. Clinton Arnold, *Power and Magic: The Concept of Power in Ephesians* (Grand Rapids, Mich.: Baker, 1997), 20–28.

2. Catherine Clark Kroeger and Richard Clark Kroeger, *I Suffer Not a Woman: Rethinking 1 Timothy 2:11–15 in Light of Ancient Evidence* (Grand Rapids, Mich.: Baker, 1992).

3. W. Bauer, *A Greek-English Lexicon of the New Testament and Other Early Christian Literature*, 2nd ed. (Chicago: University of Chicago Press, 1979), 121.

4. F. Danker, ed., *A Greek-English Lexicon of the New Testament and Other Early Christian Literature*, 3rd ed. (Chicago: University of Chicago Press, 2000), 241.

5. Wayne Grudem, in *Recovering Biblical Manhood and Womanhood*, 425–68.

6. Manfred Brauch, *The Hard Sayings of Paul* (Downers Grove, Ill.: Inter-Varsity, 1989), 261, 262.

7. John Calvin, *Calvin's Commentaries* (Grand Rapids, Mich.: Baker, 1979), vol. 21, 68–69.

8. Ibid., vol. 20, 470.

9. Clarence Boomsma, *Male and Female* (Grand Rapids, Mich.: Baker, 1993), 81.

10. Thorsten Moritz, *A Profound Mystery: The Use of the Old Testament in Ephesians* (Leiden: Brill, 1996), 56–86.

11. Leon Morris, "Adam," in *Evangelical Dictionary of Theology*, 2nd ed., ed. W. Elwell (Grand Rapids, Mich.: Baker, 2001).

Chapter 9: The Long Journey Back to Eden

1. Ronald Kydd, *Charismatic Gifts in the Early Church* (Peabody, Mass.: Hendrickson, 1984), 4.

2. Joan Morris, *The Lady Was a Bishop* (New York: Macmillan, 1973).

3. Rosemary Radford Ruether, *Women and Redemption* (Minneapolis: Fortress, 1998), 58–62.

4. Tertullian, *On the Apparel of Women*, 1.1, in *Ante-Nicene Fathers*, vol. 4, 14.

5. Augustine, *City of God*, 14.11, in *Nicene and Post-Nicene Fathers*, 1st series, vol. 2, 272.

6. Augustine, *Quaestiones in Heptateuchum*, 1:513; quoted by Kari Borresen, *Subordination and Equivalence: The Nature and Role of Women in Augustine and Thomas Aquinas*, trans. Charles Talbot (Washington, D.C.: University Press of America, 1981), 54.

7. This famous painting can be viewed online at www.christusrex.org/www1/Sistine/6-Serpent.jpg.

8. Kenneth Latourette, *A History of Christianity* (NewYork: Harper, 1953), chs. 15–25.

9. Barbara MacHaffie, *Her Story* (Philadelphia: Fortress, 1986), 94.

10. Ibid., 96.

11. Ruth Tucker, *Guardians of the Great Commission* (Grand Rapids, Mich.: Zondervan, 1988).

12. *Dictionary of Christianity in America*, s.v. "Charlotte ('Lottie') Diggs Moon."

13. Quoted by MacHaffie, *Her Story*, 106.

14. Ibid., 109–110.

15. Ibid., 114.

16. Maureen Fitzgerald, foreword to *The Woman's Bible*, by Elizabeth Cady Stanton (Boston: Northeastern University Press, 1993), vii-xxxiv.

17. Dean Hoge and Jacqueline Wenger, *Evolving Visions of the Priesthood* (Collegeville, Minn.: Liturgical Press, 2003).

Chapter 10: Understanding the Times

1. Lesslie Newbigin, *Truth to Tell* (Grand Rapids, Mich.: Eerdmans, 1991), 85.

2. Rebecca Merrill Groothuis, *Women Caught in the Conflict* (Eugene, Ore.: Wipf & Stock, 1997), 25–26; David Olson and Amy Olson, *Empowered Couples* (Minneapolis: Life Innovations, 2000), 72; Diana Garland, *Family Ministry* (Downers Grove, Ill.: InterVarsity, 1999), 200–201.

3. James Orr, *Progress of Dogma* (London: James Clark, 1901).

Scripture Index

Subject Index

We want to hear from you. Please send your comments about this book to us in care of zreview@zondervan.com. Thank you.

ZONDERVAN™

GRAND RAPIDS, MICHIGAN 49530 USA

WWW.ZONDERVAN.COM